Live Your Life

Gail Felton

ISBN: 978-0-6151-6586-8

Table of Contents

Acknowledgements and Introduction...

I'd like to thank my daughter Tami for being there when I needed a shoulder to lean on and whose light shines on me every day. *She also gave me the incentive to write this book. My son-in-law, Robert, helped and encouraged me throughout the process.* **My companion, Larry gave me the space to accomplish what I needed to do.** *I would also like to thank my sisters--Cynthia for allowing me to use the journal that* **Mom wrote in everyday.** *(This book was given to her when we all separated things after* **Mom passed).** *Thank you, Donna—for being that bug in my ear—telling me things were going to be all right; Nisey (Denise), for her kind and giving ways and words of wisdom; and Lenny (Lynn), for just being Lenny—for listening to all my gripes and for unknowingly giving me the title of this book. I'd also like to thank Maryanne— who worked with* **Mom, became more like a daughter to her—and became a part of our family.** *I owe my brother Billy (William) a special thanks. He purchased the computer that started me off, he has helped me in more ways than I can remember, and he was always there when I needed him.* I was "that rock" for all of them. That's what I wanted everyone to see.

Little did they know what I was going through. Mom meant so very much to me (Not that she did not mean the same to everyone else).

In the time I spent with Mom, we shared so many things. We used to dream so much. Sometimes I miss her so much it hurts. Writing this book was hard for me. It opened up so many wounds which only God can help me heal...

Chapter 1

The First airplane ride

My mother, Hazel Williams, was sixty-four years old, and she was going to Disney World in Florida for the first time. I called her in the morning to let her know when my husband, Vincent, and I would be by to pick her up to take us to the airport. She said she had put her bags by the front door last night and that she would be ready. Mom had been talking about our trip for a couple of weeks.

It took about forty-five minutes to drive to the Philadelphia International Airport from her house and we live two blocks away from Mom. My husband dropped us off to check our luggage, and he parked the car. While the two of us sat and waited, Mom said that getting on the airplane frightened her. She had never flown before. I told her there was nothing to worry about. Even though she was afraid, nothing was going to stop her from flying. She really wanted to see Disney World, and she didn't want to miss her granddaughter's graduation. The real reason was that the three of us were going to Florida was because my daughter was graduating in December from Florida State University in Tallahassee. My only child, Tami, was receiving a Master's degree in English.

Mom told us that she didn't want to sit by the window. We seated her there anyway. I've known my mother all my life, and I knew that once in the air she would come around--and she did. While in the air Mom reluctantly looked out the window and was amazed at how small the objects on the ground were. She found it interesting when the plane flew above the clouds. She smiled, as if she couldn't believe she was so far above the Earth. We flew from Philly to Atlanta first. Then, after a two-hour layover, we took connecting flight to Orlando Florida. This time, Mom insisted on the window seat. "I don't want to miss anything," she said, excited.

When we were on the ground, Mom was emphatic about renting a big car. She always loved the feeling of riding in a spacious vehicle. So, we decided on a white Lincoln Town Car, the largest car available.

I had visited Disney World two times before, once when Tami was a little girl and once when she was a teenager. I was filled with happiness sharing this experience with my mother. The twenty-fifth was about one week away, but I wanted this trip to feel like Christmas. It took a long time for us to get to our hotel.

Our hotel was only a few miles from the amusement park. Everyone was tired, so we unpacked and then had a late dinner at a restaurant down the road. After eating, I called Tami to let her know we made it to Florida than we settled into our room and drifted off to sleep.

We were up early the next morning. It was cloudy and dreary. As I looked out the window at the steadily pouring rain, I felt a little disappointed. But, we decided not to let the weather interfere with our plans to take Mom to the park. We got ourselves together, and drove to Disney World. It was raining even harder now so we stopped at the gift shop before entering the park to buy something to shield us from the rain. We wound up purchasing three bright yellow Mickey Mouse ponchos from a gift shop near the entrance of the park where we sat on a bench waiting for the park to open.

When the park opened, we started walking through the entrance, only stopping to purchase a book of tickets. I could feel the butterflies in my mother's stomach when she stepped through the gates and Disney World spread out before her. She is tall, lean and looks younger than her years. I have four sisters and one brother, and she could be our older sister.

Vincent suggested riding the monorail first, and then we could decide where to go from there. As we were mapping out our day, the sun came peeking through the clouds. We removed our rain ponchos, folded them, and placed them in my backpack.

After almost an hour walk in the park, Mom said her knee was hurting and she was tired so she wanted to find a spot to sit for a while. I thought this unusual and it concerned me, since Mom loves to walk and shop. The weekend before our trip, she was out shopping with Nisey, one of my younger sisters, starting early morning to late that Saturday evening. We stopped for about fifteen minutes until she was ready to walk again.

We started at the Enchanted Tiki Room in the Magic Kingdom, where there were birds with long beaks suspended from the ceiling and on swings. Bird carvings

4

covered the walls. Then suddenly, the birds started to sing, even the ones in the wall, filling the room with music. Mom was surprised when the birds in the walls started to sing; I could tell she loved being there.

I can't remember the name of the next ride or what part of the park it was, but we walked into a large room with rows of long benches, sat down and waited for the room to fill with people. When the room filled, the light dimmed and the benches started moving. In the front of the room, prehistoric animals ate from tall trees in what felt like a rain forest. I think Mom enjoyed this ride the best.

Next, we boarded the Sky Line, which carried us high above the park. Mom didn't want to go at first. She said she was afraid of heights. Reluctantly, she got in, sat down, and held on to me with her eyes half closed. At the highest point, however, Mom opened her eyes and started pointing excitedly at all the places we had visited earlier. Later, while at Epcot, we had the chance to try different foods from all over the world at the food courts. We tried stir-fried vegetables from Japan, Vincent and Mom had bratwurst and beer from

Germany. We topped it off with a tasty assortment of Norwegian pastries.

Mom took everything in like Tami did the first time she was at Disney World. Our stay in the park lasted all day. We did not leave until well after dark that evening. Before leaving the park, Mom said to Vincent, "We've seen everything." Why did she say that?" I thought to myself.

He immediately mentioned all the things we had missed. Nonetheless, by that time, Mom's knees were hurting so badly that she was ready to go back to our suite and relax. Vincent dropped us off at the room. He then went back to Disney World to do more exploring. After he left, I said to Mom, "Never say to Vincent 'we've seen everything,' because you can rest assured he will tell you that you haven't."

Mom kept talking about the plane ride, the park, and just the fact she was out of the house and in another state. We talked as we got ready for bed. All evening, she said she was tired. Mom did look tired, so I said that I was going to go into the other room and go to bed so she could get some rest.

The next day we were going to drive to Tallahassee in the Town Car. That evening, we were invited to a reception hosted by the department chair where Tami worked at Florida State University.

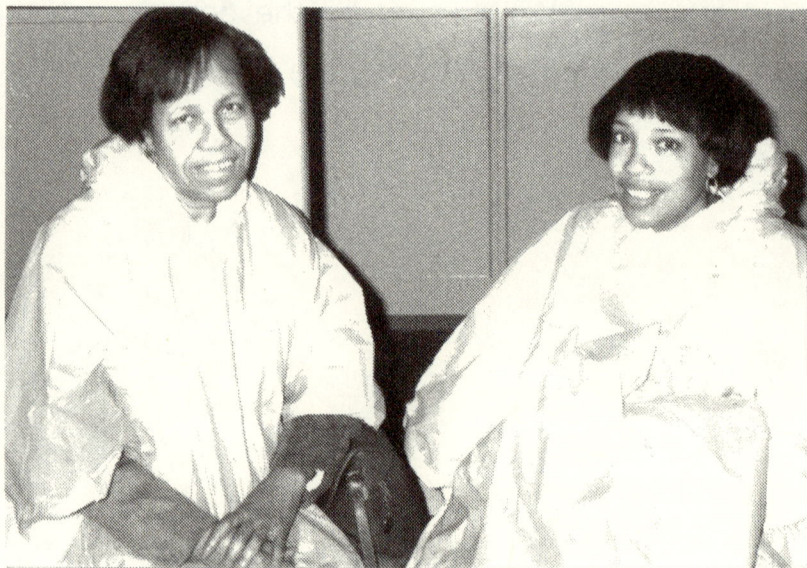

Mom and Gail in Disney World, Orlando, Florida

Mom, Vincent and Gail

Vincent had gotten up to take yet more pictures of the new hotels and some other things. By the time he returned to the room, Mom and I were dressed, packed, and ready to go. He wanted to get still more pictures of the park, so he drove us back to Disney World. Mom and I sat in the car while he took more pictures of things he missed last night and that morning. Mom and I waited for him for about ten minutes.

It took only a couple of hours to drive from Orlando to Tallahassee. The hotel we stayed in was downtown. Mom was still not feeling well. She said in addition to being tired her stomach was hurting.

The first thing we did was visit Tami at her apartment. Her place was a small two-room efficiency apartment with a kitchen the size of a closet. Mom commented on how "cute" it was. Tami's stuff was packed because she was coming back home with us after the graduation. I told Tami how proud I was of her as we drive back to our hotel room.

We then picked up sandwiches for lunch, returned to our rooms to eat and relax before the reception, which was to be in a few hours. Tam, Mom and I talked until it was time to get dressed for the party. Tam was dressed so I went into the next room with Vincent, leaving Mom to change for the party and Tam sat watching television. After I was dressed, I came into Mom's room to find her stretched out on the couch and staring silently off into space and Tam dozing beside her. I left the room before they noticed me. I combed my hair and after about ten minutes of silence, Mom came into our room to tell us she was not feeling well and that we should go to the party without her. She wanted to rest and prepare for the graduation ceremony tomorrow. We didn't want to leave her in the room alone, but she said she would be fine. I told her we would not stay too long at the party.

I thought at first, maybe we were pushing Mom too hard. I could see in her face that she was not feeling well and she looked tired but I wished Mom had come with us to the reception. Everyone at the party wanted to meet Tami's grandmother. There was lots of good food and handouts, mostly candy. I didn't think I could be any prouder of my daughter as she introduced us to her friends. I told the host that Mom was not feeling well and wanted to rest up for the graduation tomorrow. We stayed for about two hours.

Before coming back to the hotel, we swung by to pick up Tami's luggage and brought her back with us. Thinking about Mom, I was uncomfortable all evening.

We brought back a platter of food, which I placed in the refrigerator. There was chocolate and other goodies. Mom was asleep so I didn't wake her. I placed the candy on the table beside her so she would see it when she woke up tomorrow morning. In my nightgown, I sat on the side of the bed for a while wondering why my mother was not feeling well. Tami turned the light out in the next room. As she settled into bed beside Mom, I hoped Mom would be okay for the graduation. I then said my prayers and went to bed.

The graduation ceremony was long, just as we expected. I was so proud when Tam's name was called we clapped and yelled the loudest. We also took lots of pictures and videos. Though she was not complaining, I could tell Mom was tired. She was excited for her granddaughter, but I knew that the ceremony was much too long for her. When everything was over, we took more pictures.

After the graduation, we were all invited to a reception at Robert's parent's house. Robert had been Tami's boyfriend for about three years. We ate and mingled with more of their friends. After everyone had eaten, Tami and Robert opened their graduation gifts in the living room.

I asked Mom how she was doing. With a little discomfort in her face, she said she was glad to be here. There was not a word about feeling bad the entire day, and I don't think anyone else noticed.

We were the last to leave Willie and Don (Robert's parents) and on the way out, we said goodbye and thanks to everyone.

The next morning we flew back to Philadelphia. Mom really liked flying. I enjoyed the trip, but it felt so good to be home again. We had dropped Mom off at her home. I called her to see how she felt. The tone of her voice told me that she was not much better. She mentioned her stomach again, so I thought it was something she had eaten. I figured she would be fine after resting.

Vincent and I usually had an open house before Christmas every year, but we were tired and only had two days to get everything together and the tree wasn't even up. Vincent and I talked about it and decided not to break the tradition. My sisters and brother all live between Philadelphia and Jersey. Vincent's family also lives in New Jersey and Philly. As always, we invited both families and our closest friends.

Whenever we have a party, Mom was usually there before everyone else to help us prepare the food. This Christmas she didn't show up until well after the party begun. She said she still had stomach pain so I gave her two of my Zantac pills, which I take for reflux or a sour stomach. The medicine didn't work, so she went home. The party was over an hour or so after Mom left. We all wanted to take Mom to the emergency room, but she did not want to go. The next day when I called to see how she felt, Mom told me she was feeling a little better.

Robert with his Mother, Willie

Tami with Mom

Mom, Tami and me

Chapter 2

Rectal Cancer

The holiday had ended, and it was now Saturday, January 2, 1993. Mom had invited Vincent, Tam, Nisey, one of my sisters four years younger than I, Lenny, five years younger, Matthew, Nisey's youngest son who is 5 years old, and I to her home for dinner. She was feeling better and wanted to prepare dinner for us. I went over Mom's early to help with the food and set the table. She lives about one mile away from Vincent and me, so I usually walk to her house. I have my own key, so I let myself in. She was in the kitchen basting the chicken.

When I walked in the door, she told me she was glad to see me. I washed my hands and immediately started getting the potatoes together to mash. As Mom opened the door to the oven to place the chicken inside, she said, "Gail, this will be the last big dinner I will be cooking."

I stopped what I was doing to look into her eyes. She had a serious expression on her face. She said she was still tired and continued what she was doing. I grabbed the masher out of the drawer in front of me and began preparing the potatoes. As I went into the refrigerator to get the butter and milk to add to the potatoes, a strange feeling came over me as if something was wrong but I couldn't put my finger on it.

Suddenly, there was a knock at the kitchen door. It was Nisey and Matthew. Mom used the back door most of the time rather than the front because she is almost always in the kitchen cooking or in the breakfast room eating and watching the television. She hardly ever sat in the living room.

Vincent and Tam came shortly after Nisey and Matthew, and Lenny came later. Dinner was ready before they arrived, so Nisey helped me set the table. Everyone gathered around the table to hold hands to bless the food. We started eating. Mom didn't eat much. In fact, she didn't get a plate. She just nibbled here and there.

She loved to cook and entertain the family at her home. When we had our family gatherings at Nisey's, she almost always brought a dish she prepared and the food was always delicious. After dinner, I cleared the table to make room for dessert, which was cheesecake. Mom's cheesecake was the best. She often asked us to come over and she would surprise us with something she had cooked or baked that she knew was our favorite dish. We never left Mom's empty-handed. She always tried to find something to give to us even if it was just leftover food or a piece of clothing, she thought we might like. I remember her giving me a flowery housedress, which I really didn't like but I took it anyway and stored it in my drawer.

After dessert, I helped Mom wash the dishes so she wouldn't have to clean up after we left. We knew Mom enjoyed having us over, but no one lingered that day because Mom said she wanted to relax. When I got home, I called her and she said she was washing a small load of clothes. She also told me that she wanted to rest the remainder of the evening. I asked if I could come back to keep her company and help with the wash. She said no and that she did not feel like talking.

I thought she was acting strange, but I wanted to give her space.

I called again later that evening to let Mom know we had a good time at dinner. I was really calling to find out if she was okay. She said she was still tired and wanted to get to bed early, so we didn't talk long.

The next day, when Mom and I talked on the phone, I could tell by her voice that she wasn't feeling well. Mom never complained, but I could always tell when things were not up to par and she was not herself. She had been this way since after our Florida trip. We used to be on the phone for hours talking about nothing and everything. And now, Mom wanted to rest all the time.

The next morning, Tam had a doctor's appointment. She wanted to find out why she had more than usual monthly cramps. She had not seen a doctor in quite some time. At least not since she left high school and started Hampton University then graduated school about six years ago. I stopped by to see Mom at the University of Pennsylvania where she started working in the Harrison Research, in the 1960's into the 90's than Student Financial Services where her friend

Mary Anne also worked. Mom worked at the University of Pennsylvania for a total of twenty-five years. I had been working at the school in the College office, in the same building with Mom for five years. Lenny worked across the hall from Mom, in The College of General Studies (CGS) so we would have lunch together almost every day.

I visited Mom at her office and noticed lots of mail on her desk and Mom looked as if she really did not feel like working. While the university was closed during Christmas week; there was a week's worth of mail to separate and distribute. She was trying to play catch-up and clear her desk as much as she could. She would be leaving early for a doctor's appointment, which was scheduled at 2:00 p.m. that afternoon.

Mom wanted to find out from her doctor why she has been so tired and why her stomach and knees were causing so much pain. The doctor examined her, drew blood, and scheduled an MRI of her knee for Monday, January 11. After her appointment, she went home, started dinner, and went upstairs to change into another one of her flowery housedresses. Comfortable, she came back downstairs to check on the leftover chicken and cabbage she placed in the convection oven before going upstairs. When it was ready, she sat down to eat, and then turned on the television to listen to the news. After eating, she washed the dishes and swept the kitchen floor. She shut off the television and made sure the front and back doors were locked. Then she headed upstairs to her bedroom to relax.

First, she sat on the side of the bed for a few minutes and then decided to watch television so she reached over to the other side of her bed to get the remote for the television. Just then she started having stomach cramps again, so she went to the bathroom. That's when she noticed she was hemorrhaging from her rectum. This frightened her, so she called me.

I asked if she had gone to her appointment and, if so, did she mention the stomach pain and cramping to her doctor. She said she had. The doctor said he would know more after he gets the test results. She wanted me to call my doctor to set up an appointment to find out why she was bleeding. The doctor Mom was referring to was someone I was seeing for my digestive problem that I have had for a few years. I hung up the phone and called my doctor to explain to him that Mom was bleeding from her rectum. He told me to tell her to go directly to the hospital emergency room, ask them to do a blood workup and endoscope and he told her do not leave until they find the problem. I ran to her house where she was ready and waiting for me at the door, we got into her car and I drove her directly to the emergency room.

We didn't have to wait long in the emergency room. A nurse drew more blood and the doctor said she had hemorrhoids, and they could not find anything else wrong. They said go home, and "If you have any other problems come back." We were there from 8:30 p.m. to 11:00 p.m. so I took Mom home and stayed with her for a while until she was ready to go to bed.

It snowed the next day, Saturday, January 9. The telephone woke me up. It was Mom telling me she woke up with a bloody nightgown and sheets and she didn't know what to do. I told her to wait there and I would go to the hospital again with her. She said that she would go alone and she was already walking out the door. Mom wanted me to let my sisters and brother know where she was in case they tried to reach her and she would keep me posted. This worried me so I called my oldest sister, Cynthia, and asked her to let everyone know that Mom had gone to the hospital and that I was going to meet her there. I couldn't just stay at home and wait for her call; I was too anxious.

When I walked in the hospital emergency room, I saw Mom. She had already checked in and was waiting for them to call her name. As I sat down next to her, she looked at me and said she was relieved I was there. We sat quietly for ten minutes before Mom said she had to go to the bathroom. About 3 seconds after she closed the bathroom door, it came open and she stuck her head out of the cracked bathroom door and asked me to come in. She had started hemorrhaging again and it wouldn't stop. I called the resident into the bathroom to show him that Mom was bleeding again and I had strong suspicions it was not just hemorrhoids.

The nurse told Mom she would be admitted as soon as a bed became available on the floor. While waiting in the examining room for a half hour, Mom started hemorrhaging again. By then, it was 11:30 in the morning and her room was finally ready. Mom was assigned room 493 bed, no. 2 on the fourth floor. A doctor came in to examine her, a nurse took her vital signs and placed an IV in her arm. While in emergency and before a bed was available, the nurse asked Mom if she had any allergies as she placed an ID bracelet on

Mom's wrist. The testing started shortly after Mom was admitted. I was surprised because tests are hardly ever done on the weekend unless it's a real emergency. They told her she would not be able to eat or drink, not even water, until they finished testing and all the test results were in. I called everyone to let them know where we are and to bring Mom some slippers and/or socks because she said her feet were cold.

A few years prior, I spoke with Mom about the problems I was going through with my reflux, IBC (irregular bowel syndrome) which for some reason at age 7; it was hard for me to digest certain foods. Eating meats was a particular problem I guess, because I ate very quickly and didn't chew my food very well. I mentioned to Mom that she should see my doctor to get a colonoscopy I started becoming aware of my health problems in my adult life and started to take care of my health issues. I told her that he is a very good doctor. But when Mom asked me how old he is and I said he was my age, she said she did not want to see him because she felt he was too young. I did not push it, but I wish that I had. I never mentioned this to Mom again, but I'm sorry now that I didn't push more for her to get a colonoscopy.

Early Monday morning, Cynthia and I visited Mom in the hospital. We visited early because we wanted to speak with the doctor about Mom's test results. The nurse at the station said the attending doctor would be up to speak with us within the hour. Cynthia and I went into Mom's room to wait. After about half an hour, the doctor walked into the room slowly, looked at Mom, me, then at Cynthia and back at Mom. He said the diagnosis was carcinoma of the rectum, which meant Mom had rectal cancer. The doctor also said she was at stage III. This meant the cancer has spread to nearby lymph nodes, but it had not spread to other parts of her body.

He said surgery should be done immediately because the cancer was in her rectum. He said to make sure they could get all of the cancer they would had to reroute her large intestine and give her a stoma/colostomy. The pathology department would have to look at the tissues to determine how much chemotherapy and radiation she would have to get after examining the tissue. She would have to wear a pouch for the rest of her life. Not too many options, I thought to myself as I listened to the doctor explain the details of the procedure to us. It felt like this was something I was hearing on a movie and it wasn't real, this can't be happening to our Mom.

Once the doctor finished talking, Cynthia looked at Mom to ask her how she felt about this and Mom said," I want to live."

Surgery was scheduled for Thursday, January 14, at 8 a.m., the doctor said, and while he was talking, Cynthia and I could not take our eyes off Mom. I tried not to look at my sister because I didn't want to lose control and start crying. While in a daze after hearing this news, I heard Mom say, "Well, I guess I will have to have surgery right away then," after the doctor gave us the details, he asked if we had any questions. We didn't so he left the room. Someone came in to get insurance information from Mom. While Mom spoke to the women regarding her insurance coverage, Cynthia and I excused ourselves, telling Mom that we were going to the cafeteria to get something to eat.

Neither of us was hungry, but we needed an excuse or something to get out of the room fast! While walking to the cafeteria, we could not help or keep from crying when the doctor's words were sinking in. The thought of our mother having cancer was just too overwhelming. My first thought was that Mom's life was over.

We were gone for just ten minutes and when we returned to Mom's room, we made sure there were no signs of tears in our eyes so Mom would not know that we had been crying. When we returned to the room, Mom was alone. Cynthia asked her how she felt about the surgery. Before Mom had the chance to think about Cynthia's question or to answer her, the phone rang. It was Tami with the results of her test. She told us she was scheduled for surgery on Thursday, January 14, for complications due to endometriosis.

Tami spoke with Mom for a while, telling her about her test results but Mom did not say too much about her diagnosis. Then Mom handed the phone to me. I told Tami about Mom's diagnosis, surgery and that Mom was also scheduled surgery on the same day. I was trying to digest the information about Mom and her surgery, then Tami told me she is going in for surgery on the same day. I felt torn because I wanted to be with Mom and my daughter Tami.

Mom's room soon filled with the deliveries of cards and flowers. Vincent, Tam and I sent flowers. She also received flowers from one of her coworkers, Sharon. A work-study student from the department where she worked, William, also sent flowers. There were also lots of cards from her department at the University where she worked. All of these gestures made her smile.

Cynthia and I stayed with Mom until late that evening. At the end of the day, I was tired and felt as if a part of me was ripped out of my body without my permission. On the way home on the train, all I could think about was Mom, the Cancer, Tam with endometriosis and both having surgery on the same day and I could not be at both places at the same time.

Lord why is this happening
to me. I still have so much to
do before I die.

Mom, Nisey and Mary Anne at Nisey's for a cookout

Chapter 3

Care, Giving, and Learning

Thursday, January 14, Nisey's birthday and the day Mom and Tami were to have surgery. I wanted to be with both Mom and Tami but they were scheduled to be at two different hospitals forty-five minutes away from each other. My sisters and brother planned to be with Mom, and I would stay with Tami. We kept in touch by phone.

Mom was taken down to surgery at 8:00 a.m. and Tam at 8:30 a.m. I managed to get the phone number in the surgical waiting area at Mom's hospital when I visited the day before.

It took only an hour for Tam's surgery, so before I knew it, the waiting room receptionist said Tam had gone down to recovery and I would be allowed to see her in about an hour. I waited a couple of hours before calling Cynthia at the hospital to get the stats on Mom. When I called, I asked the person who answered the phone if there was someone in the waiting area named Cynthia. I heard her place the receiver down and about a minute later, Cynthia picked up the receiver and said they were the only family in the waiting room and she did not have any news of Mom's condition yet. I said Tami was in recovery and I would be able to see her soon.

While talking to Cynthia, I heard the receptionist in the background tell everyone that Mom's surgery had gone well and she was also taken to recovery but didn't give a time when they would be able to see her. Cynthia told me to hold on so she could get more information about Mom. I heard the receptionist in the waiting room tell Cynthia that Mom went to recovery in stable condition, and the doctor would be down shortly to speak with the family.

After I got off the phone with Cynthia, Tami's surgeon came down to speak with me. He said Tami should be feeling a lot better and hopefully she would not experiencing any more painful monthly cramps. He also said that if she plans to have children she should not wait but start trying right away once she's married.

I stayed with Tam for the remainder of the day and decided I'd see Mom the following day when she would be more alert and aware of me being there. My sisters and brother stayed with Mom until late that evening waiting for her to be taken to her room before leaving.

The next day, I visited Mom early and was surprised to see her awake. Her eyebrows lifted and her eyes widened when she saw me in the doorway. I walked over to her and gave her a big kiss on her forehead the way I used to kiss my grandma when I was a child and I caught her sleeping in the living chair when I came home from school. Mom was hooked up to two IV's, one in each arm, and there was a tube from her nose down to her stomach. She was catheterized with an oxygen tube strung around each ear with two openings in the tube to let out oxygen for her to breathe. I could see that the tubes made it difficult for her to speak but her wide smile told me she was glad to see me. As Mom lay in her hospital bed, I thought of how helpless she looked. The sad part was that there was nothing any one of us could do. But I was so glad the surgery was over and I know Mom was too.

As I sat in the chair beside Mom, I heard voices in the hall. I got out of my chair and peeked out into the hall to see the doctors flocked together. I assumed they were discussing the charts they were holding. I came back into the room, adjusted the sheet and spread on the bed for Mom, and sat down again. The doctors' voices suddenly stopped and I assumed they would be starting their rounds. While I was talking to Mom, the nurse came into the room to draw blood for more tests and the technician took her vital signs.

Dr. Richard Morrow, Mom's surgeon finally walked into the room. There were two other doctors, who followed him which I presumed were residents. I introduced myself to them, then he explained to Mom and I how the surgery had gone and what she should expect the next few months. He told us he'd given her two units of blood and seven lymph nodes were removed to help stop the cancer spreading to other parts of her body. Dr. Morrow said she was in stage three of cancer. At this stage, the cancer had spread to four or more nearby lymph nodes but not to any other parts of her body.

He said during the surgery they had to reroute her large intestine, which she knew would happen, and gave her a stoma. He reminded us that this process could not be reversed. He called it an ostomy. The reason for this was the cancer was in her rectum so they had to cut, suture, and close her rectum. She would have to undergo chemotherapy and radiation in a few weeks. A nurse would be visiting Mom at home to take her vital signs for a couple of weeks to check on the her incisions and to check Mom's pressure because it had been usually high. The nurse would also change the dressing on her wound each visit.

The chemotherapy treatment will begin on Friday, February 12, less than a month after her surgery and continue for the next six weeks, three days a week. Mom would have to go through so much in order to beat this horrible disease.

As I listened to Dr. Morrow, I wanted to hold Mom and never let her go. I could not imagine life without Mom. I always felt Mom would be in my life forever. I wanted her to live until she was very old and say that she had lived her life and was ready to go. Life doesn't actually go by our plans, I thought to myself.

Dr. Morrow told Mom she would not be allowed out of her bed for the rest of the week. He said he wanted to wait until he was sure she was strong enough and the sutures had time to heal properly before resuming her regular activities.

A few days later, the tube in Mom's nose was removed. The doctor wanted her to continue with the oxygen, which she didn't mind. She said she liked breathing fresh air. One IV line was removed which made her feel good not to wheel an extra pole around when she was allowed out of bed. Everyone visited so I did not stay long because I wanted to see Tami for a few hours. I knew that Mom would be all right with Donna, Cynthia and everyone there.

When I reached the hospital, Tami was asleep. As I sat in the chair beside her for a few hours watching TV and thinking about Mom, I realized I was not paying much attention to my daughter. I was fatigued from running between hospitals and worried about Mom and the cancer, Tam not being able to conceive and not spending more time with Tami or Mom. When Tam finally woke up, I helped her up in the bed and positioned her pillow so that she would be more comfortable. I then turned toward Tam, telling her I was sorry I had not been as receptive as I should have been for her.

The dinner tray came up shortly after we began talking. She ate, we hugged, she told me it was OK and I told her I would try to do better. A few hours had gone by when I heard the announcement that visiting hours were over but I still sat for a while talking to Tami's roommate who also had surgery for endometriosis.

Seconds later I heard footsteps in the hall that stopped at the doorway of Tam's room. Tam did not see them at first, but when we finally caught a glance of the two people in the doorway, she was so elated. They were friends from college, Kerri, who lived in Virginia, and Kira was from Maryland. They lived in the same dorm together for two years at Hampton University.

The hospital staff was going through a shift change, so the new nurse who would be caring for Tami came into the room and introduced herself. At the same time, Tami introduced Kerri, Kira and me to the nurse. After a few minutes, the same nurse came back into the room to tell us that she was sorry but visiting hours were over. Tami told the nurse that her friends had just arrived and were from out of town. The nurse said since they had come from so far away, her visitors could stay the night as long as they were quiet and Tam's roommate didn't mind. I was glad they came. I gave them all a hug and left the hospital feeling happy my Tami would not have to spend the night alone. It was ironic that they were so much alike in more ways than I think they knew. Tam was released from the hospital the next day.

A few weeks had gone by and Dr. Morrow came into Mom's room to tell her she would be able to go home on Wednesday. It was Sunday and she was happy to hear the news, of course.

On the morning Mom was to leave the hospital, I came early to help her pack her belongings. Mom had spent 18 long days in the hospital. We waited in the hospital room to be picked up by the ambulance. Mom mentioned her bottom hurt when she sat too long. I told her it was probably from the surgery and it should go away soon. At 10:30 a.m., two men wheeled a stretcher into the room.

Mom said her goodbyes to the hospital staff than I helped over to the stretcher, she got on, laid down and one of the men strapped her in. When we got to the ambulance the other man put Mom's bags in the back of the van and he directed me to front of the van.

I heard the back door of the van shut and we were now finally ready to go home.

The drive was short; we were home within 15 minutes. As the men wheeled Mom on the stretcher into her house, Mom said she was embarrassed. The neighbors watched as they had parked her on the sidewalk in front of her house. I watched as they checked to make sure the straps were secure, I got out of the van to unlock the front door to the house as the two men rolled Mom up the outside steps into the house and up the stairs to her second-floor bedroom. I left Mom on the bed and walked the men to the door, thanked them, and they were gone. I locked the door behind me and went back upstairs. Mom was very tired so I helped her to change into comfortable clothes. Then she sat in a chair by the window and looked at me and said, "I am happy to be home."

Mom was settled in at home, sitting upstairs in her bedroom in her favorite wingback chair by the window. She said she was still tired but essentially fine. We all decided to take one day per week to care for Mom. Since there were 6 of us, we alternated the weekends. Billy, my brother and oldest sibling, brought us to and from Mom's whenever we needed to be there. It was a very cold, snowy and icy winter so it was hard for some of us to get there even by car. We all were fortunate to be able to be away from our jobs one day a week; my day was Tuesday. We stayed at Mom's for the day and spent the night and waited for the next person to relieve us before leaving that next evening.

The visiting nurse came early the next morning to take Mom's vital signs and change the dressings. Mom kept telling the nurse how tired she was and that her rectum where she was sutured always hurt when she sat in the chair. The nurse said she will be sore for a while. She was also experiencing pain in her lower back. Mom wanted to stay in bed most of the time. We prepared her meals and brought them up to her because we didn't think she was ready to tackle the steps.

Tami was feeling better so we went over to Mom's to hang out. Nisey and Matthew had spent the night and were still there. Mom stayed in bed most of Sunday. Cynthia brought food over: chicken, string beans, and potatoes. Cynthia enjoyed preparing lots of food on Sundays. Lenny, my youngest sister brought over greens and as usual, she only made enough greens for half the people at Mom's so we would tease her, including Mom, about preparing so little for so many of us since Mom loves her greens but they were never enough.

The following Monday, Mom asked the nurse to look at her stitches to find out why she was hurting so much. The nurse found a small opening in her rectum that should have been closed at the time of her surgery. The nurse said that I should make an appointment with her doctor to get the opening sutured.

The next day was February 5, Cynthia's birthday. Mom called her at 6:45 a.m. to wish her a happy birthday. She always called early to be the first one to give a happy birthday wish to her children. She apologized to Cynthia for not getting her a card for her birthday this year.

Mom had an early appointment that day to close her incision from her surgery. I took her to that appointment and after the procedure, which was done as an outpatient, she asked the doctors to explain again about her treatments. She also wanted to know how she would feel once they started the treatment and the starting dates of the chemotherapy and radiation treatments. She was anxious at the thought of going through the treatments and didn't like the fact that she might lose her hair. We listened for quite a while to the doctor as he answered Mom's questions. It was so much information to digest. I could see that Mom was tired but she wanted to know what she had to do to get rid of this terrible disease.

Mom always felt more comfortable when one of us went with her to a doctor appointment so we could explain to her clearly just what the doctor had said in layman's terms. Mom was not able to hear clearly in one ear, but hardly ever wore her hearing aid, even though it would improve her hearing. In fact, she gave it to Cynthia who has had hearing problems since she was a child. Cynthia actually needs two, one for each ear. I think maybe it was because she was a premature baby (7 months) and her eardrums probably never had the chance to fully develop. Donna, my sister a year older than I, as children used to pretend to speak to Cynthia, mouthing words but not making a sound. Cynthia would ask, Donna, "What did you say?" Donna and I both knew she had hearing problem, that's why we did it. Children can be cruel sometimes.

Billy, the oldest of Mom's children and the only boy, came over early the following Sunday morning with fresh fish. I was there with Mom since it was my day to care for her. When he rang the bell I ran down to let him in. He placed the fish on the counter in the kitchen, went upstairs where Mom lay in bed, and sat in the chair. During the visit, he told Mom she should get out of bed and fry the fish. He stayed for an hour and left. I was annoyed because Mom was getting angry at him telling her she needed to get up and out of her bed to cook.

Mom told me she felt guilty after he left so she decided to get up to fry the fish, and it was good! Cynthia stopped by with corn muffins. Nisey and Donna also came over. Donna lives in New Jersey and Billy lived just around the corner from Mom.

Cynthia and I both lived about a mile from Mom in opposite directions; Lenny, the youngest of us all, was just a bus ride away. I called Mom the next day even though I had a migraine headache, I didn't care. It felt good to talk with her about everything and anything again. I hadn't done this for what seemed like quite a while. I missed our long talks on the phone. We used to talk for hours. After almost four weeks, I felt Mom was beginning to come around and she seemed to be almost herself, aside from being very tired most of the time. The rest of the weekend she rested up and didn't do too much of anything, since she knew she would have to deal with her treatments in a couple of days.

Mom went on short-term disability from her job at the University of Pennsylvania starting January 24, 1993.

I long for you to call to say I am missed,
thought of and loved.
I miss being held when I am troubled,
listened to when I need to talk.
The feeling of emptiness in my heart is back
once again.

Chapter 4

The Long Haul

On a snowy Friday in February, I went to the hospital with Mom for her 10 a.m. appointment. She was scheduled for a pelvic scan, blood work, and her first chemotherapy treatment. At the hospital, we went directly to x-ray where she was to have her pelvic scan. We sat in the waiting room for a long time. The receptionist finally asked if Mom had other tests scheduled because she said the x-ray department was backed up and running about forty-five minutes behind schedule. I told her Mom was scheduled for blood work and chemotherapy. She told us to get the blood drawn then come back.

By the time we returned to the x-ray department, we only had to wait a few minutes before Mom's name was called for a pelvic scan. The scanning process did not take long and we were finished by noon. Her first chemotherapy treatment was scheduled for 2:15 p.m.

The chemotherapy treatment was also late; we sat waiting for a while until they started the drip at 3:15 p.m., which lasted two hours. When Mom was finished with her treatment, we left the hospital. On the way home we stopped at the market to pick up a few things Mom said she needed for the house. We didn't get home until 7:30 p.m. Mom had such a long day and was weary. When we got home, we ate leftover fish and string beans for dinner. After dinner Mom said she wanted to go to bed. Mom went up to bed while I cleaned and swept the kitchen and breakfast room floor. When I finished downstairs, I came upstairs and Mom was in bed asleep. It actually worked out well that her treatment was on Friday. This gave her the chance to relax during the weekend before her next treatment.

The visiting nurse helped Mom for about two weeks and Tuesday, February 9, was her last day. Mom was doing things on her own now and said she was glad she didn't have to get up early and go downstairs to wait for the nurse to arrive to open the door. After today she will be able to stay in bed late and get up when she is ready. For some reason, I felt it would be a long haul on her road to recovery because it was difficult for her to walk from the front bedroom to the back bedroom without getting very tired. Tami stopped by to sit and chat a bit with Mom. She stayed for five hours and went home. Mom told me that evening that she really enjoyed her visit with Tami.

Sunday was Valentine's Day. We all came over to see Mom with plates/dishes of food. Not expecting the company, she was glad when she saw us. A few friends were there as well. It turned out to be a nice day. Even the weather cooperated.

Mom's next appointment was at 2:30 p.m. on Monday, for her second treatment of chemotherapy. She would receive her treatments of radiation when the chemo treatments were over. Each time Mom had her chemotherapy treatment she was very tired. That evening, as I sat in the wingback chair near the window in Mom's bedroom, I listened to Mom as she told me about her day and the young child who sat beside her having chemotherapy at the same time. Still listening, I got up and lay beside Mom on the bed. Mom looked at me to say "I was complaining about having to go through chemotherapy and radiation . . . and, you know, I've had a chance at life, this child has not yet lived." I agreed with what she'd just said. She rolled over and closed her eyes and I then got up to wash and prepare myself for bed. When I finished in the bathroom, I pulled the blanket back beside Mom, to lie down, and, before I knew it, we were both asleep.

In the days that followed, Mom went through many bouts of nausea, vomiting, and weakness from the chemotherapy. She had a difficult time keeping food in her stomach. She began to lose lots of weight, so the doctors decided to discontinue the chemo to see if the nausea would go away and she would be able to eat.

On March 19, Mom was scheduled for an outpatient appointment to get a port placed in her chest. This was suggested since her veins were always hard to find during her chemo treatments. It would also make it easier for the lab to get blood before each treatment without constantly poking at her arm to find a vein. Chemotherapy was continued on March 30, with a combination of 5-FU and another chemo drug, called

Leucovorin. It was a regimen of six weeks on and two weeks off.

After the chemotherapy treatments were completed, two weeks went by before it was time for radiation. Again we all took turns going with Mom to get her treatments. My day was still Tuesday. After Mom received her first week of radiation treatment, and didn't get nauseous or sick, she decided to try to do things on her own. So, she called for hospital transport whenever she needed to go for her treatments. She said she needed the space. We had to respect her wishes.

When the radiation treatments started, it was administered five days a week; the total schedule of treatments was to be thirty. Mom seemed to be doing well and she has almost completed all of the scheduled radiation treatments. One evening Cynthia called Mom to see how her day went and how she was feeling after her the treatment. After hanging up from talking with Mom, Cynthia called me to say that Mom sounds weak and her voice sounded as it she had been crying. She was due to have her last treatment of radiation the following week. Cynthia wanted me to find out if what she was hearing was correct. I called Mom, and I noticed her voice sounded weak. After hanging up with Mom I called Cynthia back and told her that Mom's voice was weak and that she trailed off a couple times while on the phone.

Cynthia and I met at Mom's 20 minutes later. We didn't want to call anyone until we found out what was going on. When we arrived, we went directly upstairs to find Mom sitting in her favorite chair by her bedroom window. She did not look well, so we told her we were going to take her to the hospital emergency room. She was still dressed so I got her jacket and helped her put it on. Immediately after, we were out the door, into the car and I was driving her to the hospital. Cynthia thought perhaps Mom was dehydrated. Mom never complained when she was in pain or didn't feel well, nor was she giving us much information. When we reached the hospital, they got a wheel chair for Mom then took her vital signs. The nurse said Mom was in fact dehydrated and needed IV fluids. They directed us to a room with an empty bed and gave Mom a hospital gown to change into, placed and ID bracelet on her and admitted her right away to find out why she is dehydrated.

As we helped Mom undress to change into her hospital garment, Cynthia and I both noticed Mom was burnt badly on both of her inner thighs between her legs. We asked the nurse about it and she said it was probably from the radiation. Apparently, she was given too much and did not tell the technician it was burning. Of course this made me angry with Mom because she should speak up if she is not feeling well or the radiation was burning her. Mom was supposed to have thirty treatments of radiation, and she wanted to have all thirty treatments regardless of the third-degree burns. She had the twenty-ninth treatment that day. She felt that if she received the amount of treatment the doctor ordered, the cancer would be gone.

We felt relieved that Mom was in a place where she could get the care she needed. They were treating her burns before we left. We gave Mom a kiss and told her we would be back tomorrow. When we got home, Cynthia and I called everyone to give them the details of what had happened and the reason for Mom having to stay in the hospital.

The Doctor who sent Mom for her radiation treatments saw Mom the next day and determined that she had been over-radiated, and most of her intestines were cooked. So, the doctor decided she would not get her last radiation treatments.

She was nauseous and vomited all the time. A gastric tube had to be put in her nose down to her stomach to pump out all the bile in there causing her to be nauseous. The reason Mom was unable to eat food was because she had so many kinks in her intestines from the extensive radiation treatments. Eating caused nausea and occasionally vomiting. Off and on for a few months Mom had good days and bad -- mostly bad. She had two surgeries to try to correct the kinks in her bowel, but it didn't seem to help.

Mom's doctor suggested she speak to a nutritionist, which she did a week later. The nutritionist suggested that Mom have surgery again to place yet another port near her collarbone for tube feeding. This process of feeding was called TPN--Total Parental Nutrition. She would have to feed everyday, 12 hours a day, overnight and into the morning.

A few days after the second surgery, the nutritionist showed us how to connect Mom up for her night feedings. We wanted to learn so we could take care of Mom ourselves and she would be able come home. The next day was a question and answer session with my sisters and me. Billy really did not want to be involved in this. He wanted to be the person who transported us from our homes to Mom when we were unable to make it in bad weather.

After the session Lenny and Nisey decided they did not want to participate in this process, but would be there to help if Donna, Cynthia, or I needed it. I hated that Mom had to go through this and I hated the fact the technician didn't notice the burns on Mom's thighs when Mom had her radiation treatments.

The lessons started a couple days after the nutritionist talked to us. Cynthia and I attended the first lesson. I videotaped it while the nurse showed us step by step what had to be done. The nurse who instructed us was Maureen. She set Mom up for feeding in the hospital. The second lesson was the next day. It was just Donna and I, because Cynthia had an obligation at her job.

I thought if we had any problem once Mom was home, we could look at the videotape to see what was going wrong. I found out that it wasn't that easy. The feeding pump, pole, and other equipment had to be ordered and in place in her bedroom before they let us bring Mom home. Maureen had to set up the feeding pump. Supplies such as tubes and syringes would have to be delivered once a week as well as the feeding bags containing vitamins Mom was lacking since she was unable to eat without nausea and vomiting. Mom was finally released from the hospital a few days after our training sessions.

We took turns caring for Mom. A visiting nurse came once a day to take vial signs, and to make sure everything was going well with the feeding pump, and make sure the port was not infected. We learned how to flush the tubing and check Mom's blood for sugar. I hated sticking Mom's finger. Every time I asked which finger she wanted me to use, she held her hands up to look at all of her bruised finger tips, looked up at me, and said "It doesn't matter." We also took her temperature, measured her urine, give her medications, and jotted down her progress in a book. I remember the nutritionist telling Mom before Mom left the hospital she would never eat again. This left a bad taste in her mouth.

We all pulled together to nurse Mom back to health. Every now and then, we would have our meetings to talk about how Mom was progressing and if we had any concerns. We also discussed who would have the time to care for Mom on the weekends. That's when we decided to alternate. After realizing she would need more time than she thought to recover, Mom decided to retire for medical reasons. On September 1, 1993, my mother had worked for the University for 26 years.

The beginning of January, 1994, around the fourth, it was my turn to stay with Mom. I had a problem that night with the kinks in the tubing, which I tried to straighten but the pump kept beeping and I couldn't find the problem. I had to disconnect and flush the line. I telephoned one of Mom's nurses, Barbara. She said to not to worry about Mom's feeding and she would come in the morning to make sure everything was okay with the port and tubing. Mom was happy that night she didn't have to be tethered to the feeding tube and she slept well. The problems with kinks in the tubing and air in the line went on for all of six months before we all got the hang of it and then were able to get Mom hooked up to feeding with our eyes closed.

About seven months went by with no problems, and then Mom started having stomach pains, chills, and nausea. We called her nurse, and she suggested we take Mom to the emergency room. After I hung up the phone another nurse came by to make sure Mom was all right since she had a house visit with another patient nearby. She said she was not supposed to do this but she wanted to drive Mom to the hospital while I drove Mom's car with Donna in the passenger seat beside me and followed her to the hospital. The roads were icy and she drove an SUV. The nurse made sure Mom was checked in before she left us so we didn't have to wait long in the emergency waiting room. Mom was given a series of tests, which showed yet another obstructed bowel and an infection in the port. The next day, Mom went into surgery again. They had to replace the port for feeding. The port was moved from the left side of her chest to the right. They replaced the central line and two days later she had surgery to straighten out the kinks in her colon. This new line would be good for a couple of years since she had to continue her tube feeding the rest of her life to maintain her weight and to get the proper nutrients. The doctors had to remove more of her intestine and did a resection to correct the obstruction, which left her with a short bowel.

That night after the surgery, Mom lay in the hospital bed in her room, and prayed to God to take the pain. Mom was allergic to most pain medications. She had a high tolerance for pain and was given extra strength Tylenol after each of her surgeries. Suddenly, she saw three figures wearing white robes, standing in a bright light. She wasn't sure if this was a dream or if this was real. She said to them she wanted God to take away her pain. The figures stood there for about 15 seconds, and then disappeared. After they were gone, so was her pain.

She told me this story the next day.

Mom was released from the hospital and things ran pretty much okay for the next few months. Every now and then Mom would place an orange slice in her mouth (without the advisement of her doctor), chewed it, and spit it out just to get the feel of chewing and the taste. She was careful not to swallow. Mom did this for sixteen months. She often said whatever was in the TPN made her feel as if she was having hot flashes and night sweats. After a few months the nutritionist realized it was the sugar. Most of the sugar was removed, and Mom stopped having night sweats and hot flashes.

Tami called Mom on January 1, 1995, to let her know that Robert had proposed to her and they would be married the following October. Mom was so excited for them. She really liked Robert and was happy to hear they were getting married.

More months went by and Mom started chewing small amounts of food, meats and fruit mostly, and spitting it out, just to get the taste of food in her mouth. She hoped she would be strong enough to attend Tam and Rob's wedding. Things started getting a little better for Mom over the next few months. She was always talking about the wedding, wanting to go shopping to find something to wear.

I was on the phone with her constantly because she wanted help choosing an outfit. She was thinner than she had ever been, but said she felt well enough to attend the wedding on October 7, 1995.

The day of the wedding, Mom danced and looked so happy. She wore a black dress with a black and gold long vest. That was the best we'd seen her in a long time. She even posed for a few pictures. We all had such a good time. Tami made a beautiful bride and

Robert a handsome groom. This day was truly a good
day for us all, especially Mom.

> God has given you more
> than you have hoped to bear

> Although the cross is
> heavy, the path long

> God is good and He'll make
> a way.

58

Mom, Tami, Neil and Robert

Mom and me dancing at the Wedding

Tami

Chapter 5

Getting there

Mom had a routine appointment to see Dr. Richard Rosen, her gastrointestinal doctor. While there, he recommended she talk with Dr. Rolondo Rolendelli at Hahnemann University Hospital who specialized in gastrointestinal disorders. She was happy about this because it gave her hope. She called to make an appointment and it was scheduled for a week later.

After the first visit, Mom felt comfortable with Dr. Rolendelli. She said he is a warm patient person, which was very rare in doctors. She said he would ask her if she had any questions and he would take the time to explain things, and made sure she understood before continuing to another topic.

Mom worked with a nutritionist Dr. Rollendelli recommended to develop a different food regimen. Mom suffered from diarrhea, pain and cramping in her lower abdomen. Four grams of Questran was prescribed to help with the diarrhea and Peptamen to maintain her weight. Even though she was able to eat only small amounts of food, Dr. Rollendelli said she had short bowel syndrome and her intestine was not able to absorb vitamins. She had to have some type of food supplement.

Peptamen and Questran came in cans, which were delivered to her house every two weeks along with plastic hanging bags with tubing. Each night she "ate" two cans of liquid through her IV, which took eight hours to empty. Mom was 5 foot, 8 inches, and her ideal body weight was approximately 125 pounds. Her present weight was 101 pounds.

After a few months, Mom told Dr. Rolendelli that she started having pain in her abdomen again. It was still difficult for her to maintain her weight because of diarrhea. Dr. Rolendelli discovered after more tests that she had a small block in her colon, and he would have to perform a small bypass, which he wanted to do as soon as possible. After a while Mom was able to eat small potions of food.

Mom, however, had planned to go on a cruise with Nisey and Matthew the last week of August and into September. Dr. Rolendelli agreed it would be OK to wait until she returned. She was looking forward to it very much. The trip was an eight day-seven night cruise to Cozumel, Mexico, the Grand Cayman Islands, and Jamaica. Mom wanted to postpone the surgery until after she returned in September. I came over to Mom's one evening two days before they were scheduled to leave to help her pack for the trip. She found it interesting when I showed her how to roll her clothes to save space in her suitcase. I had to go to work the next day so my visit wasn't long.

Mom, Nisey and Matthew had to fly to Miami, Florida to board the ship. This was the second trip and the third flight on an airplane for Mom. Once they got on the cruise ship, Mom was so excited and wanted to relax and start her vacation. Mom asked Dr. Rolendelli before she left about food. He told her to try to eat as much as she could in small amounts and it would be okay. Out of the three places they visited while on their cruise, Mom enjoyed Cozumel the best. She loved the blue clear water and white beaches. She also enjoyed the mini tour in the small boats called tenders. Jamaica on the other hand, she said, was much too hot and humid for her taste. But, she had lots of fun meeting interesting people who she stayed in touch with by mail.

Mom returned from the cruise weighing approximately 102 pounds--up from 99 pounds before the trip. She was still thin and not so happy about the continuing nighttime feedings. Her abdomen was mildly distended, so Dr. Rolendelli ordered another scan to look at the problem. The CAT scan showed an obstruction in her small bowel, which he had suspected, and a hernia.

On September 6, Mom had a scheduled appointment to see Dr. Rolendelli. This visit was to talk about the upcoming surgery to repair the hernia, do an exploratory laparoscopy, and get rid of the adhesions. Hopefully this would also restore some of her small bowel function. He said he would try to work with a plastic surgeon using some of her stomach muscle to form a bridge to stop her gut from kinking. After mapping out all the details, the date of the surgery was scheduled for September 11, 1996.

On the day of the surgery, I drove Mom to the hospital early since I had stayed with Mom that evening and everyone met us there. We all waited with her in the waiting room. After about ten minutes, she was called. Each of us gave her a kiss, and then she followed the receptionist through a set of double doors. Her surgery was scheduled for 8 a.m., and it was almost that time.

We read, talked, and reminisced about our youth to pass the time. Before going into surgery Dr. Rolendelli came in the waiting area dressed in his scrubs. He said he would be working with another doctor (plastic surgeon) and together they would try to fix Mom so she will be able to eat food (larger amounts) again without pain, cramps, etc. It was as if God had sent Dr. Rolendelli to us to care for Mom; he truly is an excellent doctor.

Donna suggested that we hold hands and pray. She started with a few words, and then each of us added a line or two to the prayer.

After a couple of hours, Dr. Rolendelli walked through the twin doors. We all huddled close to hear what he had to say. He explained the procedure and where they were with the surgery. He asked the receptionist for a piece of paper to draw a diagram of what was done and what was left to do. He showed us where he left about a foot of small bowel in Mom's GI tract, which rescued some small bowel and should allow her to have better absorption. A tube was also placed to open her bowel. He said the adhesions were eliminated. The small bowel resection and the hernia still had to be repaired. The plastic surgeon, Dr. Rolendelli said, was now working to remove a portion of Mom's stomach muscles to support the remaining colon. This should help stop kinking and blocking.

When Dr. Rolendelli was finished explaining the procedure to us he returned to the operating room. There was a feeling of relief that Mom was in such good hands. Dr. Rolendelli cared about our Mom as he did all of his patients and we trusted him completely. We were all glad that he was there for her.

Mom had a problem with the anesthesia. She didn't wake up right away. So, after they were able to wake her, she was sent to the Post Anesthesia Care Unit for a few hours before going to recovery. We were not supposed to see Mom right away, but Dr. Rolendelli made it possible for us to visit her in the recovery room for just one minute, two of us at a time. I was just grateful to see her for a brief moment. We all took a deep breath after we saw Mom and she was all right and in good hands, then we all went home.

The next day, when we visited Mom, she was awake but didn't speak much. She had a tube in her nose down to her stomach. She was catheterized and had lots of monitoring devices and equipment around her.

After eleven days in the hospital, most of the monitoring devices were removed. Mom was given clear liquids, which she tolerated well. Her bowel functions returned, and she was feeling better. She was recovering nicely.

Mom was finally advanced to a soft diet. They continued with her tube feedings to make sure she was getting the vitamins her body needed. Before we knew it, Mom was finally tolerating a regular diet, in small amounts but larger than before the surgery. The tube feeding was decreased, and Mom was released from the hospital with a follow-up appointment with Dr. Rolendelli in two weeks.

March 1997 Tam announced she was pregnant with the due date in August. Every chance I got I'd visit Tam and Robert, staying the weekend to help ready things for the baby. I wanted to be there when Tami delivered and to help out as much as I could with the new baby.

When Tam and Rob went for an ultrasound a few months later, Vincent and I were also there. Robert and Tami agreed to let us know the sex of the child as long as we didn't tell them or anyone else. Vincent and I were both curious. The ultrasound took place in a small dark room. The technician asked Tami and Rob again if they wanted to know the sex of the baby. They said no, but it was okay to let Vincent and I know. After the technician completed the ultrasound, Tam and Rob turned their heads, the technician mouthed to us the sex of the baby. I was so excited. That was the hardest secret I ever had to keep.

Mom would repeatedly ask Tam about the name she would choose to call the baby at the same time wanting to get from me the information about the baby's sex. Tam and Rob were careful not to tell anyone, not even me, the name they had chosen for the baby, at least not until he/she was born. They selected a girl and a boy's name. Mom told Tam and Rob, she didn't want her to name the baby a name she would not remember or couldn't pronounce. Tam smiled at Mom and said, "It's an English name if a boy, it will be easy to pronounce; and the girl's name will also be easy for you to remember and pronounce, Mum-Mum (the name Mom was called by her grandchildren). You will be able to pronounce either name."

August came in a blink. Tami was working at the Discovery Theater at the Smithsonian Institution. Her coworkers gave her a surprise baby shower, and they called me a week before to see if I would be able to come to surprise Tam and of course I said yes. I will finally get the chance to meet her coworkers and put faces with the voices I had spoken to on the phone every now and then. So I made arrangements with

Robert to pick me up from the train station without Tami knowing and take me to the surprise baby shower.

The day of the shower after Rob dropped me off; I had time before Tam arrived to meet some of her co-workers. When Tami finally walked in the shower everyone yelled "Surprise!" She had no idea they planned a party for her. She always said, "I'm a hard person to surprise because I can sense things." She kept asking how I was able to keep this secret from her, I told her it was very hard. As we walked around the room, she introduced me to other people she worked with from her old department at the Smithsonian Associates as well as her current department. This was also Tam's last day of work. Her delivery was in a couple of days on August 16.

A couple days before the delivery date, I visited Tam and Rob so I could help them prepare for the baby's arrival. Rob assembled the crib, which was a gift from Vincent and I from a shower I gave Tam a few weeks ago to invite the family in Philly. Tami and I placed the fitted sheet on the mattress and the blanket, (which was a shower gift from my sister Nisey) in the crib. We were able to spend lots of quality time together talking and watching movies, which I enjoyed very much. Tami was tired and couldn't wait to deliver but didn't want to be induced.

I had been in Virginia for four days and I decided to go home to take care of few things, mail etc. then return on the next day.

When I returned the following day, I was happy I did not miss the delivery. Early the next morning, at 4 a.m., Robert came into my room to tell me Tam had been having pains for a couple of hours and she said she was ready to go to the hospital. He had already called the hospital. I got dressed while Rob took her bag down and placed it in the trunk of the car. I helped Tami down the stairs and into the car to go to the hospital.

When we arrived at the hospital, Robert got out of the car first to get a wheelchair for Tami to wheel her to the nurse's station. After reaching the nurse's station, a nurse came from behind the counter to lead Tam and me down the hall to the birthing room while Robert stayed behind to fill out paperwork and give medical history information to the other nurse for Tami to be admitted. After collecting the medical information from

Robert the nurse came in the birthing room with information on a wristband to wear. Tami wanted to have the baby naturally without an IV or pain medication, but while in the birthing room the nurse insisted that an IV drip was hospital policy even with natural birth. So, reluctantly, Tam allowed her to place the IV in her arm. After the nurse left the room, I wanted to rub Tam's back but she didn't want me to touch her. Instead, Tam wanted to meditate. Rob, I could tell, wanted to help and didn't like that Tam was in pain but Rob stayed out of her way.

He was in and out of the birthing room asking every now and then if there was something he could do to help. At 10:22, on August 22, 1997, our first grandson, Freeman, was born. He was the most beautiful baby boy I've ever seen. Robert was so excited when he called his parents. I heard him tell his Mom, in an anxious voice, "We have a boy!" Vincent was there a few minutes after she delivered.

Seven days later, on August 29, after 28 years of marriage, I separated from Vincent. I moved in an apartment two blocks from our home, where I stayed for a year, then moved to another apartment forty-five minutes away. Two years later we were divorced. I married Vincent a year after graduating from high school and had never been on my own. So it felt good to finally be on my own and not having to check with anyone when I decide to do anything at the last minute. Mom was doing very well now for a year, eating without nausea or stomach cramps.

Dr. Rolendelli left Hahnemann Hospital in October of 1998 and joined the staff at Temple University Hospital as Chief of Surgery on November 1, 1998.

By March 1999, Dr. Rolendelli formed a support group with about a dozen of his patients and others, including myself. The group met the third Thursday of each month from 7 p.m. to 8:30 p.m. at Temple hospital where Dr. Rolendelli worked. On occasions, different people joined the group to discuss their surgeries, experiences with illiostomy, colostomy and other health issues since Dr. Rolendelli was everyone's surgeon he was there to explain things to us as well as answer any questions.

After meeting for a few weeks, we decided to call the group "Gut Reaction Support Group." Dr. Rolendelli attended every meeting, except for one time when he had late surgery. He popped by afterward and stayed for a bit, though. Nancy, who was the coordinator of the group, lined up the speakers for each meeting.

Mom looked forward to going to the meetings and seeing everyone. Mom's weight was stable at between 110 and 112 pounds. She ate well and did pretty much what she wanted to do thanks to Dr. Rolendelli.

In May, about a year and a half after the birth of Freeman, Tam told me she thought she might be pregnant again. She had an appointment to see her doctor on the following day. She didn't want me to tell anyone until she was sure. Of course, I was so excited when her doctor confirmed that she was indeed pregnant. Again, Tam and Rob did not want to know the sex of this baby.

Freeman was almost two years old and this would be the perfect time, I thought, since Tam and Robert wanted three children because their next baby and Freeman would have two years between them. Mom was so excited when Tam told her about the pregnancy. Mom was always going to Atlantic City, staying over

Nisey's for a small cookout or just going out shopping with Nisey.

Acting as if life owes you
something is a sad thing

Wanting more out of life
than just existing is a good
thing.

Chapter 6

Breast/Lung Cancer

Early in December, 1999, Mom was preparing to go to Atlantic City for a weekend stay, which she did every now and then when she felt lucky. Saturday morning at 10 a.m., I walked over to her house to visit her before she left. I let myself in and called up to her to let her know that I had arrived. She was upstairs in her bedroom preparing for her trip.

As I sat in the chair by the window, I heard her say "Ouch!" in a nonchalant way. She was washing under her arms and breast, and felt a couple of lumps. She said that area where she had just touched was sore. I walked over to her while she was standing at the bathroom mirror and watch her as she ran her fingers over the lumps under her breast again. She looked up at me and said "It's very tender in this area." Then she took my hand and placed it under her left breast for me to feel. There were two lumps about the size of marbles. Even though she tried not to show it, I saw the shock in her face. She said she wasn't going to worry because she had just had a mammogram four months ago in August and the results were normal.

To tell you the truth, I was concerned. She continued getting dressed and a few minutes later she grabbed her bag and went down the stairs as I followed. She locked up the house, we got in her car, and I drove her to the bus stop. I watched her as she got on the bus that was parked in a parking lot while a lot of senior citizens fumbled to find their ticket to board the bus. After she got on the bus she sat in a seat by the window, she looked out at me and smiled. I waved good-bye as the bus pulled off, thinking about the lumps under her breast. I parked the car in front of her house and walked home. After I got home, I called my sisters Donna and Cynthia via conference call to tell them about the lumps and how Mom brushed it off. They were also concerned.

The day Mom returned from Atlantic City, we called her one at a time trying to convince her to go to the doctor to get the lumps under her breast looked at by a specialist. Dr. Rolendelli was on vacation so she didn't want to see or talk with anyone until she had the chance to talk with him because she trusted him and wanted him to suggest a specialist.

A couple days later, Tam started having false labor pains. I packed my bag to go to Virginia to help her since it was close to her delivery date. Two days after I arrived, Tam started having real labor pains. This time we knew what to do. We got in the car, I took care of Freeman, who was now two years old and Robert had his hands full with Tam and her bag for the hospital. We knew the hospital drill. Rob grabbed a wheelchair when we reached the hospital, Tami was able to fill out some paperwork this time and then they directed us to one of the birthing rooms. Tami refused to go with their policy of placing an IV in her arm this time.

Tam's doctor stopped by to check how far she was dilated and to make sure Tam was okay. About a half hour after the doctor left the room, Tam told me to get Robert, he was in the next room watching television and keeping Freeman busy. She had just come from the bathroom and told me to call the nurse in the room. One nurse came into the room and a few seconds later another. The first nurse wanted to check to see if Tam was ready to deliver but when she saw the head of the baby she called a doctor. She said to the other nurse, "She's ready!" the nurse said, smiling. Before the nurse could get everything together and before the doctor arrived, the baby was born. We all stood staring down at the baby, saying nothing, our mouths wide open. Freeman was even amazed at the delivery. He laid his hand on one of the nurse's shoulders and carefully pushed her out of the way to see what was happening. Tami shouted, "Is my baby all right?" the nurse said yes and a second later the room became busy. Robert, Freeman, and I moved out of the way to give the doctor space when he arrived to take care of the new baby and mother.

On December 15, 1999, at 3:03 p.m. our second grandson was born. He was named Isaac. There was another beautiful, beautiful boy. I called Mom to let her know she was a great mum-mum for the fourth time. My sister Cynthia's daughter, Nadenia, has a son by the name of Ricardo, six years old. Lenny's son David has a son named Talon, one year old, who was Mom's third great grandson. Mom was so excited. I stayed for another day after Isaac was born and came home to see what was happening with Mom. Vincent came down for a couple of days and Robert's mom was there for Tam this time to help her with the new baby. His parents had driven up from Florida to stay until after Christmas. I was planning to return to Tam and Rob's during the Christmas holiday.

When Dr. Rolendelli returned from his vacation, he recommended a breast specialist and surgeon in his hospital for Mom. The specialist told Mom on December 19 that it might be cancer.

The breast cancer specialist suggested that Mom have surgery to remove the lumps under her left breast and to get the tissue analyzed. Mom wanted to wait until after the holiday to have the surgery. January 19, 2000, was the date of the surgery. Two lumps were found, both cancer, one 1.8 x 1.5 x1 cm. and the other lump measured 1.5 x 0.8 x 0.9 cm. They were about the size of marbles.

When Mom received the diagnosis, she cried. She said she was not angry, just sad. She wanted to continue moving on with her life.

ON Dec 8, 1999 ✓

I First Relize I had Breast
CA, I was prepaning to go to
AC. Happy (About 10 AM)
I Ran my hand over my chest
my left Breast was Soke
    I Remember Raising my Left
Arm A small Lump About the size
of A Marble was there on the under
side of my Breast (I "Knew" it was
CA) - I was Shock
    On the 15th of Dec I was
told it was possible CA

    On the 19th of Jan 2000 I
had Surgery it was Two Lump
Both CA one 1.5 and 1.8 Center
Meter in size

    On August 8th 1999 I had
Breast Mamogram

Mom wrote this note to herself after she was diagnosed with breast cancer

The Surgical Pathology Report read "A Radical mastectomy, removal of the left breast and lymph nodes." Her surgeon suggested radiation treatments. Mom had chemotherapy but, refused radiation for two reasons. First, because of the other radiation treatment she had for her colon, which had cooked her intestines causing her to be on the feeding pump for the rest of her life. And, because she felt it was too close to her heart, and she didn't want to damage it like it did her colon. Her recovery wasn't as long as the other surgeries. She bounced back fairly quickly.

A few months had gone by. My daughter and her husband celebrated their fifth wedding anniversary on October 7, 2000. They made arrangements to go to a hotel for the weekend. Mom and I were invited to stay and sit with the boys at their home in Virginia. Freeman was three and Isaac was almost year.

For the three days we were there, at any given time, Mom would sit in the kitchen with her chair close to the sliding doors reading O magazine. She always watched the Oprah Winfrey Show, hoping one day to meet Oprah. Mom called Tami every day to watch

Oprah together and discuss her guests over the phone. Freeman stayed close to Mom, and Isaac always wanted to be around me. He reminds me so much of Tam when she was a child, always wanting me close by.

Freeman wanted to show Mum-Mum something downstairs in his playroom. When they got to the bottom of the stairs, there was a large bug. Mom got so excited and wanted to kill it. Freeman said, "It's a cricket Mum-Mum!" For months after we got home Mom would bring this incident up and laugh about it.

Mom and I had fun going out for lunch and taking a walk down the road with the boys that weekend. When Tam and Rob returned they told us it was such a nice getaway weekend and thanked us for staying with the boys. We took the train back to Philly the next morning.

The following August, I invited Mom over to my house for what she thought would be a jewelry sale in the meeting room in the apartment complex where I lived. We had planned a 70th birthday party for her and everyone was there and waiting for her to arrive. Her birthday was August 4 and mine was August 31. Mom never liked to come to any of our houses empty-handed, so when she came to my house she brought with her matching burgundy pillows with fringes for my sofa in the living room. She said it was an early birthday gift for me. Mom was in a hurry to leave to see the jewelry sale, as she thought. So we left my apartment after I placed my new throw pillows on my sofa.

The meeting house was less than a block away and I wanted to walk in the room last since I know everyone wanted to see the surprised look on Mom's face when she realized it was not a jewelry sale but a birthday party for her. I opened the door to the meeting room and told Mom to go in. Everyone yelled "Surprise!" At first she was puzzled because she had no idea why everyone was there until we starting singing happy birthday to her. She was happy and truly surprised.

She walked around the room saying "Hi" to family and coworkers she had not seen for a while. Her uncle, my great-uncle Jack who was my grandmother's brother, was able to make it at the age of 92. He was there with his nephew Reese. Reese drove Uncle Jack and his wife Viola to the party. He had survived colon and prostrate cancer only a few years prior. He had gone through chemotherapy and radiation, and was doing well. After Mom finished greeting her guests, she grabbed a plate of food and we were ready for her to open her gifts.

A trip to Las Vegas was my brother's gift to Mom. It was a place she always wanted to go. I was chosen to accompany her and our trip to Vegas was scheduled for the following week. Our trip was paid for in full by Billy.

Mom and Nancy from the Gut Reaction support group

The trip was for four nights/three days. Mom was not able to stay a week because it would be too long for her to be without her night feeding. The party went on for the next three hours. We ate and danced to the music while Mom had the chance to talk with some of the people from our Gut Reaction support group as well as old friends from University of Pennsylvania where she worked. At the end of the party, I took videos of some of the guests while they were leaving and others were candid shots of everyone talking, dancing etc. That was such a good day for all of us and I was so excited about going to Las Vegas, the first thing I did when I got home was pack.

The day of our trip, Billy met Mom and me at the train station to give us some spending money to use on the slot machines in Las Vegas. Billy said goodbye to us as we boarded the Regional Rail line train to the airport. We were booked at the Rio Grande Hotel right on the main strip where Billy had stayed a year ago on his trip to Las Vegas. The flight was smooth and wasn't a very long but when we got there it was late evening. We checked in, Mom was tired so we decided to just relax. The next morning when we opened the curtain at the window, the mountains were so beautiful. Our room was spacious. It's funny that we really didn't notice all of this last night because we were so tired. Mom and I lay in bed and talked for hours before we decided to get up. Our entire trip consisted of reminiscing, eating, gambling, and going to shows. Mom said she was really enjoying herself and wished we had a few more days to stay. On the last day we stayed up late to go to a show because we didn't have to be at the airport the next day until the early afternoon.

We really milked the last day; we had room service with breakfast in bed, talked and looked outside our window admiring the mountains. After breakfast we took our time packing and I made a call to the lobby to let them know that we needed transport service to the airport. At the airport, Mom even played the slot machines while we waited for our flight. It was the perfect birthday gift for her and for me. I'm glad Billy made it possible for me to share the Las Vegas trip with Mom; we spent so much quality time together in those three days.

When we returned home, aside from the night feedings, Mom was feeling good and things were finally going well for her. The following day I was back to work and invited my friend Larry over for dinner.

I had been dating Larry for about a year now. He is a friend I had known for many years. He got divorced about the same time I did. Larry also worked at the University years before I started, but in a different department.

On February 28, 2001, I had prepared dinner for the two of us. Shortly after dinner, I started getting gas pains in my lower abdomen. I wanted some ice cream but the pain kept getting worse and I didn't want to eat anything until the pain went away but prepared a bowl of ice cream for Larry. He asked why I was not having any and I told him I had gas from something I ate and I did want to eat another thing until the pain went away. He suggested I take something and I said I didn't want to. But, I knew eventually I would have to because the pain was getting more intense. By 1:30 a.m. the pain was unbearable. Larry called the ambulance to take me to the hospital. Larry was angry that I didn't mention the intensity of the pain sooner. The ambulance arrived within twenty minutes. The paramedics asked if I needed to be taken down on the stretcher since I live on the third floor and I said no. We took the elevator down to the first floor where the paramedic strapped me onto a stretcher and rolled me into the back of the ambulance, asking me questions and writing everything in a notepad. Larry was directed to sit up front with the driver.

The ambulance took me to the nearest hospital. Unfortunately, it was not the hospital I wanted to go to. I was glad Larry was with me, though. The pain was getting more severe, and I asked for something for the pain. The paramedic said they will run an IV line in the emergency room and will give me a pain medication once they find out why I am having pain. When we reached the hospital, I was given an IV, then taken down for x-rays of my abdomen. It was 4 a.m., so I didn't have to wait. The diagnosis came almost immediately.

The emergency room doctor said I had a bowel obstruction and would have to have surgery. They finally give me pain medication through my IV line.

Larry called Mom to tell her I was in the hospital. I specifically told him not to upset Mom and be as calm as possible. Mom had enough on her plate, and I didn't want to worry her with this. After Mom talked with Larry, she phoned Dr. Rolendelli because she wanted him to take care of me. Dr. Rolendelli than called the emergency room to arrange to have me transported by ambulance to his hospital, Temple University. Larry left me to go to work after he made sure I was OK.

I dozed off for what seemed to be an hour. When I opened my eyes there stood Dr. Rolendelli. He told me he saw the x-rays. There was a bowel obstruction and I most definitely needed surgery. Since Dr. Rolendelli was not a doctor at this hospital, he was not allowed to examine me until I was moved. After a few hours and lots of IV pain medication, I was transported to Dr. Rolendelli's hospital. I was there for a few days before I had surgery. The doctor was hoping it would pass. It didn't, so he had to proceed with the surgery.

Mom visited me almost every day. She washed my feet and gave me clean socks. Mom had lots of appointments there at the hospital for some reason. She had an infection in her port she said, for which she was given an antibiotic. Usually she visited me after her appointments.

I recovered from my surgery in two weeks; I was then able to go home. The day I went home, Dr. Rolendelli asked if I was feeling better. I wanted to be home, so I said I was even though I was still in a lot of pain. Larry came early to the hospital; he did most of my packing. I lay on the bed telling myself I'd rather be home and I'd get better when I got home. Mom and Donna came to the hospital to take me home. Donna wanted to stay with me on my first night home. I started feeling even worse that evening. Donna went to the store to pick up a few things for me to eat. When she returned, I told her I was in pain and was not feeling well. I didn't want anything to eat or drink, but she insisted late that evening I take a swallow or two of soymilk. I did. That night she held me like a baby as I heard her cry.

The next morning I felt like I did the first time I went to the hospital in the ambulance. Donna called Cynthia because I started vomiting. They called Lenny because neither Donna nor Cynthia drives. Lenny called Mom and Nisey, and they all met us at the emergency room.

They found another obstruction. Two surgeries, a month's stay in the hospital, a few days in the intensive care unit and I was feeling much better. I was home recovering with my brother and sisters' assistance. They took turns preparing food and giving me my medication. By May, I was back to work, part-time at first. In a couple of weeks I was back full-time.

Mom thought I could handle the reason she had had so many doctor appointments at the hospital where I stayed. She said the metastasis were in her lungs. She told everyone while I was in the hospital but wanted to wait until I was strong enough to digest this news. Now she would have to get chemotherapy and radiation again.

I started spending between four or five days a week at Mom's. I'd go home to pick up my mail on the weekends and sometimes I would drive Mom to my place forty-five minutes away where we'd spend the night and drive back to Mom's place to stay for the rest of the week.

Mom's first chemotherapy treatment was on May 31, 2001. Mom was hooked up to an IV. She was given Benadryl drip for 20 minutes to relax, Sofren for nausea, Cimetidine to prevent reaction from Taxol, and, finally, Taxol, which took three hours. Some of the side effects of Taxol were neuropathy, hair loss, mouth ulcers, nausea, vomiting, and diarrhea among many. The next day, Mom drove to the store to pick up a few things for the house before I got home while I was at work. She stopped at the drugstore to get her prescriptions filled. When she finally got home after doing her errands she called me at work to tell me her feet felt numb when she drove and was unable to gauge how much pressure she was putting on the gas and brake pedals. After that day, Billy, Nisey, and I started driving Mom to most of the places she wanted to go. She soon stopped driving altogether after her doctor told her she had neuropathy in her fingers and feet.

In June, Mom started losing her hair. We were on our way to a Gut Reaction Support Group meeting that evening. When I got to Mom's after work, she started combing her hair and some of it came out. She decided to just comb all of it out at once instead of waking up each morning to a pillowcase full of hair. She also noticed mouth ulcers, especially after eating walnuts, which she loved to eat after dinner. At first she thought perhaps she was allergic to walnuts until she remembered this was another side effect of the chemotherapy. The ulcers in her mouth and neuropathy in her feet and fingertips did not go away after the chemo treatments were over. At this Gut Reaction meeting, Nancy invited an art therapist to come and speak. She asked us all to draw a picture of anything and when we were finished, she placed them all on the board in front of the room. She took one drawing at a time and analyzed it. When she got to Mom's drawing, there was a female adult holding the hands of two children with flower all around them. The therapist asked Mom, how many children do you have? Mom said six and the therapist said, then why is it you only drew two children? Mom replied, "These are the two I worry about the most." Then the therapist asked what were their names, and Mom said, "I'd really rather not say."

Mom's health from this point on started to get a little rocky. She always had pain in her feet; the mouth ulcers came and went. Her MIC key button came out of her abdomen, which she needed for her nightly feeding. I drove her to the emergency room to get it replaced. They put in a Jejunostomy catheter for feeding instead. To see the doctors in emergency shove the new tubing in place and to hear Mom scream was hard. They wanted to try to do this while there was still an opening from the old tube without her going through surgery again. When they finally had it in place, they gave Mom two Tylenol and we drove home in silence.

Her feeding formula was changed to Isosource by her nutritionist, and she was told she needed to use four cans daily. After the chemotherapy she did not want to eat much because she was always nauseous.

Mom wanted to attend a Breast Cancer support group that met from 1:30 p.m. to 3 p.m. on Wednesday afternoons. She was able to take a bus that dropped her off in front of the hospital, and she wouldn't have to walk far. She attended a few sessions and then stopped because with the neuropathy, it was hard for her to get around alone. These meetings were held in a conference room in Temple Hospital where she had her surgery.

For a few months, Mom wasn't feeling well. We could tell because she was quiet most of the time, but she never complained. Thanksgiving and Christmas will soon be here and it would be a good time for all of us to get together to enjoy the holidays and for Mom to take her mind off her health issues.

Sometimes I feel like I need
to cry to relieve the pressures
within me.

The tears would act as a shield
to protect me from my sadness.

Sometimes I ask myself what
am I looking for?

I never get an answer.

Chapter 7

Christmas 2001

Mom said she didn't feel like company, so she and I celebrated Thanksgiving 2001 together. I prepared a roasted chicken with sausage stuffing for Mom and a bluefish with oyster stuffing for myself. The side dishes were potatoes with gravy, turnip greens, and macaroni with cheese. We ate by candlelight. The brownie cheesecake we had for dessert was extra special since both of us loved chocolate. Dinner was over early and we relaxed the rest of the evening. Mom was still not feeling well. Although she didn't eat much, she said she really enjoyed dinner and wanted to do the same for Christmas.

As Christmas grew near, I decided to ask everyone over to Mom's for a surprise dinner and everyone would prepare a dish to bring too. Nisey told

Mom she had a turkey she wanted to give to her to put in her freezer so we could have it when the family got together again. It was at Cynthia's, and Cynthia would bring it over when it was her turn to take Mom to chemotherapy since Billy would be driving. Mom wondered why Cynthia kept forgetting to bring the turkey over but didn't push it. The reason was, Nisey told Cynthia to keep the turkey and prepare it for Christmas. Cynthia finally told Mom she would prepare the turkey for her for Christmas and bring over some dark meat, which was Mom's favorite. She also said she would bring other foods that Mom liked so that neither Mom nor I would have to prepare a lot for our dinner together. This was so that Mom would not try to cook anything for our Christmas dinner early. Mom still was not feeling well but she was excited about making plans for the two of us to spend time together on Christmas day.

Christmas eve, I spent the night at my place. I wanted to prepare a fish to stuff and some greens to bring over for Christmas dinner. Mom assumed the reason I went home was because the fish I was going to prepared was in my freezer and the spices that I needed were at my place.

I called Mom early Christmas morning, and we talked for almost two hours while she lay in bed. I was wrapping the food I prepared last night when Lenny called me from her cell phone to let me know she was on her way to pick me up to take me to Mom's. I had moved to another part of the city, which was a good drive from where Mom lived and about twenty minutes from were Lenny lived.

After she picked me up and when we reached Mom's, we placed the food on the stove. Mom was still resting in her room upstairs. Lenny went upstairs to wish Mom a Merry Christmas and told her she had plans to have dinner with her older son, David, and his family. David lived only a few blocks from Mom. Lenny stayed at Mom's for fifteen minutes then left to visit her son.

Mom finally came downstairs after Lenny left to have breakfast. I had not had breakfast and I knew Mom was hungry, so I prepared one egg--the yolk cooked over-easy for Mom and the egg white cooked into a cheese omelet for me. We shared one slice of toast. I also made a slice of bacon for Mom and, since I'm a vegetarian, a slice of veggie bacon for myself.

After my surgery I was only able to eat small portions, otherwise I would have cramps in my abdomen.

I went upstairs to get Mom's pills as she sat at the breakfast room table watching the Christmas parade on television and having breakfast. After I finished eating, I washed the dishes, cleaned up the kitchen, and went downstairs to put a load of clothes in the machine. Mom yelled down to me to bring up two beers from the refrigerator in the basement, so we could have them with our dinner later. We both loved to have a nice cool beer with dinner.

Mom had no idea I invited the family over to have Christmas dinner at her house. Everyone was bringing something so we would have a nice variety. Whenever Mom asked everyone about what they were doing for dinner, she got the same answer that they were all having dinner at home with their families, except for Lenny having dinner with her son David and his family who lived not far away.

An hour later David and his son, Talon stopped by to see Mom. David, however, did not stay long since his wife, Chablis, was not feeling well. He wanted to get back to her. They stayed for about a half hour. When

Lenny returned, she had Billy. My brother Billy decided to bring shrimp and volunteered me to clean and cook them. So, I made shrimp scampi with rice, which turned out great. I had planned to make garlic bread too, one of Mom's favorites, but I just didn't have the time.

Nisey come with her son, Matthew, bringing with her macaroni with cheese. Donna came with her daughter, April, and son, Micah, she had prepared the salad. Cynthia brought the turkey. She was with Charles, her friend and her daughter, Nadenia, and her grandson, Ricardo. Much later, Neil, Nisey's oldest son, dropped by and Kyle, Lenny's younger son, came with his friend, Sheena.

For dessert, I made a strawberry cheesecake. Mom asked me to tuck a slice away for her to eat later. I noticed more and more while staying with Mom that she wasn't eating as much food as she used to. My mother never had a big appetite, but whenever she ate a complete meal she usually had a cold beer. After all the food was laid out on the dinning room table, we said grace and ate. All of us, Mom especially, had a fantastic day. While we were eating, she told us, it was the nicest Christmas she has had in a long time. She said this would be the last time we all would be getting together.

After she said that, I sensed that everyone felt the same way but no one responded. Mom seemed tired, but she managed to smile every now and then. We all felt something wasn't right with Mom and the way she looked. When we all used to get together Mom had so much energy. She loved mingling and talking with everyone and she would clean up this and straighten up that and always on the go. This evening, a fragile woman with so much tension on her face sat quietly among us.

Since so many of the nieces and nephews where there, we took lots of pictures of them with Mom. And, we had Mom pose for a few photos with her six children. One of the photos Donna got enlarged, made six copies, and gave us all one. It was getting late, and everyone started to leave. Cynthia and I did the dishes and put the food away.

That night I stayed with Mom. She said she hated when I had to go home, she missed me, she said she felt so lonely, but, at the same time, she wanted me to have a life. One day I said to her, "You are my life." She quickly snapped at me and said, "Don't ever say that! I am not your life!" I felt hurt. I knew Mom's time was limited and I guess that was my way of letting her know that I would be there for her as long as she needed me. She didn't know it, but she was my life.

Nisey (Denise) in the white shirt than clockwise, Lenny (Lynn), Mom (Hazel) Gail, Donna, Cynthia, and Billy (William)

Chapter 8

Brain/Spine Cancer

The nights when I stayed at my place, I called Mom and we would talk for hours about our day. When I stayed with her, we stayed up laughing and talking about old times over a box of chocolates. One time we ate two boxes of chocolates, two layers deep, in a week. And, I had the nerve to look for more when we stopped at the store to fill her prescription. Charles Whiting, who we called "Chuck" was a good friend to me and a friend of Vincent. He knew how much Mom and I enjoyed eating chocolates, so he often left boxes of chocolates (different each time) in the doorway for us to share, which I thought was such a nice thing to do, and Mom could not wait to see what was next.

A week after Christmas, on a Saturday, Nisey stopped by to see Mom. She was still in bed so I went downstairs to make our egg while she and Mom were talking. I told her I would bring breakfast up to her when it was ready and she said no, and that she will come downstairs to have breakfast at the table. It was hard for her to walk up and down the stairs with the neuropathy so I would bring it up to her before she had the chance to come downstairs. After breakfast was ready, I called to Mom to let her know to wash for breakfast. When I reached the top landing with her breakfast tray she was on her way out of the room to come downstairs for breakfast but when she saw me, she look at the breakfast tray and up at me with a smile as I was about to go into her bedroom. She said thanks but she didn't want me to wait on her and insisted on doing things for herself. Mom never ate much when she wasn't sick but I noticed, she was starting to eat even less. Mom and I sat on her bed as Nisey sat in the chair by the widow and we talked for about an hour.

When I stayed at her house, I slept in her room in the bed beside her. One night I pretended I was asleep and just observed Mom staring at the ceiling with tears in her eyes. We always slept with the bathroom light on in case there was a problem with the feeding pump so, I could see her face in the partially lit room.

I asked her why she was crying. She said she wished she wasn't so sick. I sat up, then got out of bed and turned on the lamp on the dresser closest to me. I got back in bed, and we both cried together. I reached over to get us a tissue, which was beside the box of chocolates on the dresser. I grabbed the candy, placed the box of chocolates on the bed between us. After we both dried our eyes, I offered Mom a chocolate; we chuckled, grabbed a piece and bit into the chocolate as if this would make things better. I shut the light off and we talked to each other until we went to sleep.

A week went by and by then we had eaten all of the chocolates. It was Valentines Day, so I stopped by the store at lunch to pick up some more for Mom. When I got to Mom's house, I placed them on the breakfast room table. In addition, I brought her the paper, so, I placed the paper on top of the chocolates and went upstairs to change my clothes into something more comfortable. I took the linens off Mom's bed to exchange for fresh ones. When I came downstairs, Mom had not yet seen the box of candy under the paper she was still watching the news on television. I asked her what she wanted for dinner and she said she wasn't sure. She said, whatever I prepare, she wanted very little. She took her eye off the television and looked down at the paper then picked the paper to read it. And then she saw the box of chocolates; she looked up at me, smiled and said thanks. After seeing the chocolates she said she really didn't want much dinner because she wanted to save room for her chocolates.

After dinner, we headed upstairs to her bedroom with the box of chocolates. On her way up, she asked if I would help her change the linen on her bed. I said yes knowing I'd done this earlier. It took all I had not to spoil the surprise. When she realized after she walked up the stairs and stood at the entrance of her bedroom door that there were clean sheets on her bed, she gave me another smile, looked at me and said, "You're too fast for me."

We washed up and got ready for bed. I got Mom's feeding together so that all she had to do was to connect the pump and press the start button. We sat up for a while eating chocolates until we got tired. I shut the light off and we went to sleep.

I wanted to go home and pick up my mail before going to Mom's house one day after work. My mailbox is small, so I try to pick up my mail every few days. Otherwise, the mailman shoves the mail in to try to make it fit which makes it hard for me to remove. I took one train to get to my house from work, and to get to Mom's from my place I take two trains and walked a mile to her house. When I told Mom I'd be back after I picked up my mail, she said to stay home and come tomorrow after work because she didn't feel comfortable with me walking in the dark from the train station to her house. So, I invited Larry for dinner that evening. I wanted to clear my head, plus, he was a good listener. It was a lot going on with Mom with the neuropathy; she was beginning to have memory loss every now and then, which I didn't understand nor did I like. When she mentioned to her primary doctor that sometimes she would go to the refrigerator and not remember what she was looking for he said, "I'd worry if you went to the refrigerator and didn't know what a refrigerator was," and they both had a good laugh and that was the end of it.

I prepared dinner Larry and I ate, had wine, and relaxed. About three hours later, Lenny called. She said Mom had fallen off of her chair in her bedroom while untying her shoe. She couldn't get up. Mom told Lenny not to tell me that she had fallen because she didn't want to worry me because I wanted to come over and she insisted she would be all right. Lenny called me anyway because she had to stop by my place to pick up the key to Mom's house.

By the time Lenny arrived, Mom had found a way to pick herself up from the floor. That night Lenny stayed with Mom, helped her to get ready for bed, and assisted her with connecting to the feeding pump.

I called Billy to give him an update of Mom's condition and to tell him that Mom had fallen. He insisted Mom go to the emergency room the next day. I was scheduled to be with Mom the next day, so, after work, I would go to her house by public transportation to pick up her car and drive Mom to the hospital to find out why she had fallen the night before.

I called Mom from work to tell her Billy suggested she go to the hospital. She had already spoken to him. Donna called to let me know she would meet me at Mom's so wait for her so she could ride with us to the hospital. Cynthia would go straight to the hospital from work. Lenny went home to pick up her car and meet us there. Nisey drove to work, so she would meet us at the hospital also.

When Mom, Donna and I reached the hospital, everyone was there except my brother. Billy didn't want to go to the hospital but wanted us to keep him posted. The receptionist needed a list of medications Mom was taking so Mom pulled out a piece of paper with all the information the receptionist needed. After Mom answered all the medical history and medication questions, we sat down in the waiting area, waited patiently for them to call Mom to be seen.

We waited a long time so I asked the receptionist how long it would be before Mom would be seen. He said Mom was next on the list and would be seen soon. About ten minutes later, they called for Mom. Cynthia works at a hospital, and we thought it best that she went with Mom to see the doctor since she would understand most medical terms.

Cynthia took Mom's pocketbook, helped her up and to the back where she had to change into a hospital gown. More tests were taken, mostly x-rays and blood work. We were allowed to visit Mom two at a time while she waited for the test results. We must have sat there for two hours but it seemed like twenty-four hours.

Cynthia appeared from behind the double doors, walked toward us and sat down to let us in on the test results. We all sat in a daze, listening to Cynthia. She said the x-ray showed the cancer that we thought was still in Mom's lungs, for which she was presently receiving chemotherapy, had traveled to her spine and brain. She said Mom would have to have radiation to shrink the tumors in her brain. There was silence for about twenty seconds. I wondered to myself what God's plans were.

Finally, I said that God had kept his part of the bargain. We asked to have Mom one more year after she was first diagnosed with rectal cancer, and he gave us eight. I didn't want Mom to suffer anymore. By the looks in my sisters' eyes, they were all in agreement with me.

We sat in the emergency room until a room was ready for Mom on the floor. After they gave us her room number, they grabbed her belongings and took her away. We were not allowed to go up with her because it was late, so we kissed her good-bye and said we'd be back tomorrow.

I returned the next day in the early part of the afternoon, and everyone came in one by one after me. We all took half days from work. Mom's room was noisy because she shared it with a younger person who always had visitors. When I asked Mom how she felt, she told me she could not sleep last night. The noise gave her a headache. A nurse or someone was with her roommate constantly talking through the night.

I immediately went to the nurse's station to ask for a different room for Mom. My Mom was a terminal patient with brain cancer, I explained to the nurse and the noise really bothers her. The nurse said she was on her way to a meeting, and said when she returned she would make sure Mom was moved. She was almost certain there was a private room available. Less than fifteen minutes later, when her meeting was over, she came to the doorway and waved to me to come out into the hall to say, "Don't let anyone know, she whispered, I have a private room for your Mom so please help move her out quietly. We were so grateful.

When I leaned over to tell Mom she was being moved into a private room, she managed a smile. I grabbed Mom's belongings and told everyone to help. Within ten minutes Mom was settled into her new room with the scowl gone from Mom's face. She really felt more comfortable being in her own space. For the rest of the week we all came to visit every day after work to see Mom and to find out if there was anything she needed. Saturday was Mom's third day in the hospital. I woke up early because I had planned to spend the entire day with her. I reached the hospital at 9 a.m. in case Mom needed help with bathing or just wanted company and we ended up talking the whole day. I left the hospital at 7 p.m. When I got home I called her, but she was too tired to talk. I told her I would visit tomorrow and stay again all day Sunday.

At 8 a.m. Sunday, Mom called to tell me I should stay home, relax and I could visit her the next day, Monday, after work. I was in my pajamas writing out checks and paying bills while talking to Mom. We had talked for about a half hour when her voice suddenly started to fade. Then she said, "My legs! My legs! I can't stop them from shaking." Then the line went dead. I called the hospital back immediately and the line to her room was busy. I had Mom's car since she was in the hospital, so I got dressed and drove myself to the hospital.

I reached the hospital within 35 minutes. When I got to the room, Mom was on a stretcher. The nurse said Mom had just had what they thought was a seizure but they would have to take her down to x-ray to do a brain scan to be sure.

I placed my pocketbook on the chair by the window, and went to give Mom a kiss. She said, "Gail, I never want to experience that ever again." She told me how she had lost control of her body and she had movement in her legs, which she could not control. She asked me to stay with her while at x-ray, then at that moment, her body started convulsing again without warning.

I held her close to me while the nurse called the doctor. By the time it was over the doctor was there and he prescribed a medicine to control the seizures. I looked at my watch to see how long it had lasted—it was 45 seconds. I stared at my watch instead of Mom when I heard her teeth clacking. After it was over, Mom looked up at me and squeezed my hand tightly. She said "Don't leave me. . . . Please, stay." I told her I would not leave her. I could tell she was glad I was there. I hoped never to see her like this again, but I was glad I was there for Mom. The Doctor was still there and he asked the nurse to take Mom's vital signs. The doctor said the medication would control the seizures and help her relax. He said the brain scan would not be necessary and that she would have to continue with the medicine until she receives the radiation to shrink the tumors in her brain. Then Mom could be transported to the nursing home.

A few hours later, Nisey stopped by, and then Vincent came. By this time Mom was resting quite comfortably. She didn't know they were there. I told Vincent and Nisey about Mom having the seizures and that I will be staying with Mom in the hospital overnight for as long as I can until the seizures are under control or she felt okay about being alone.

Vincent offered to bring me home to shower and to pick up a few things because I didn't feel like taking my car out of the parking garage since where I was parked was inconvenient and Vincent was parked on the street. I thought this would be a good time since Nisey could stay with Mom until I returned. Before we left, I reached over and whispered into Mom's ear that I was going home but I'd be back to stay the night and Nisey was with her. She said okay and closed her eyes again. I was only home for 20 minutes, I showered and grabbed a few items, and we were out the door.

When I returned, Mom was still asleep and Nisey was reading. Nisey stayed with me for a few hours. I told her that I'd be all right, but she insisted that I go to the cafeteria to get some food so I wouldn't have to leave Mom anymore that evening, so I did.

After Nisey left, I settled in and called Cynthia and she called Donna on a conference call. I filled them in on what had happened to Mom. I told them that I was going to stay at the hospital overnight and take the next day off from work. Donna said she would stay the following night to give me a break.

Mom slept most of that afternoon and evening. She woke up when she heard my cot being rolled into the room. She was awake for about a half hour while I made up the bed beside her.

Tam called me at the hospital that evening to ask if it would be a good idea for her and the family to visit Mom in the hospital. I told her that this would be a good time because I was not sure how long Mom would be with us.

Tam asked me if Mom had a will and I said no. She said that it is important we get this done right away. She said she would bring with her the computer program called Willmaker so we could get Mom's will together. Tam also wanted the boys to see their mum-mum and Mom to see the boys before she died.

When Tam, Robert, and the boys visited, Mom smiled. In fact, Mom always reacted that way each time she saw her grand or great-grand children.

They arrived the next day. They stayed with me only three days because Robert had to get back to work. Mom was so happy to see them. Freeman was five and Isaac three. When the boys saw Mom they gave her a kiss. They were ready to leave the hospital after a short while.

The following day, Tam called Mom from my place to tell her she wanted to help her make her will. I, of course, thought it was not a good time but Tam insisted. Tam had Mom on the phone for an hour in a half trying to get information so she could enter it into the Willmaker program. After Mom finished answering questions, Tam printed it out, gave it to me to get it notarized and signed by Mom. Tam, Rob and the boys went back to Virginia the next day.

I took the document to Mom to sign. It took Mom so long to initial and sign the entire document. Because of the medication and the brain tumor, it took a few moments to figure out what I was saying to her and where to sign the documents. The witnesses were also there to sign the document along with Mary Anne, who is a notary.

Mary Anne notarized the two sets of documents. Tam made sure everything was in order: power of attorney, medical power of attorney, and will before passing on to me. I'm truly thankful for my daughter for taking care of this.

The following day I was on a whole new mission of finding a decent nursing home for Mom. I wanted it to be near me so I could visit every day and easy for everyone to find. Lenny and I visited different facilities and also a hospice.

I told Mom about the places Lenny and I had seen. A doctor at the hospital had convinced Mom that a hospice is where a person goes to die. Mom didn't want that but she was a terminal patient and didn't understand that she was dying. Mom insisted on a nursing home. So we looked into only nursing homes.

The next day, Cynthia and I went out to find a place for Mom. We narrowed it down to two nursing homes. One was about fifteen minutes from me. The other nursing home was five minutes away. I called both places to see if they had space available for Mom and the place fifteen minutes away had an opening. Mom insisted on having a window next to her bed in the nursing home so I wanted to visit the nursing home to make sure Mom would be comfortable in this home. Mom finished her radiation treatment and she could be transported to the nursing home at any time. The following day, I visited the nursing home to see the room where Mom would be for the last time and was very satisfied with what I saw. There was an older woman in the room who was sitting up in her bed watching TV. She greeted me with a smile and hello when I walked in the room.

I was especially happy to see the large window that was not exactly beside her bed but more toward the foot and with a nice view.

Don't ponder over
The time you missed
Just enjoy the time
You had

Chapter 9

Angels are waiting

I was at the hospital early that morning, it was March 2002. I wanted to be with Mom when they transported her to the Manor Care Nursing Facility which I thought she would like because her room would be bright, sunny and she would have a window to look out when she was not in bed. I wanted to help her settle in and make sure she was comfortable in the new place. While we were waiting for the ambulance to pick us up I described the nursing home to her and she seemed pleased. When the transport service arrived we were both anxious and ready to go.

The ride to the nursing home took about forty-five minutes. At the front the building, we were met by one of the staff who told us to sign in. He led us to Mom's room. There was another person there — a roommate

— but Mom was near the window. I helped Mom unpack, putting her things where she would have easy access. Then I sat on the bed beside her.

A staff nurse came in the room to introduce herself to us. She said please let her know if there was anything we needed, and then she left the room. We were told all visitors had to sign in. The receptionist came to the room to give me the code to the front door as Mom looked around she said so far she liked her room. I was glad to hear her say this. Later that evening, Lenny came by with Billy but they didn't stay long because Mom said she was tired and wanted get to bed early. She wasn't set up for overnight feeding yet, so that would be something we would have to discuss with her nurse tomorrow. I stayed for an hour after my sister and brother had gone until after Mom got prepared for bed, I kissed Mom, said good-bye and went home.

I stayed home from work the next day. Carl, a good friend who I've known since first grade, called to see if there was anything he could do to help with Mom. I thought it would be nice if Mom had a comfortable chair by the window instead of the straight-back chair that was there at the Nursing home. I asked Carl if he would help me bring the wingback chair from Mom's house to the nursing home. It didn't take us long to pick it up and take it over. Carl stayed for a while before taking me home to pick up my car. It took me about two hours to care take of a few things at my place, and then I drove back to the nursing home to stay with Mom.

Two days later, Mom was pretty much settled in. I came to visit her after work and she looked at me with a serious face and said, "They're not very nice here." I was shocked. I thought I had done right by sending Mom there. My heart dropped into my stomach. I asked her what had happened and she said when she asked for help getting out of bed, the person who helped was rude. And, when she needed help going to the bathroom, no one responded to the call button.

I decided at that moment to camp out with my Mom in her room. I felt responsible. The reason Mom was here was because I chose this nursing home.

I called my boss, Christa, to let her know I wanted to take a couple days off to care for Mom. She said it would be fine. Prior to Mom getting sick, I hardly took any time off at my job so my boss was very understanding when I wanted to be with Mom. I went home and picked up a few things. I told Mom I'll be with her for as long as she needed me. I stayed there for two nights when Donna decided to help. Donna told me she would stay the next two nights and we would rotate.

The rest of the family pitched in except for Cynthia. Cynthia was caring for her friend who was dealing with issues relating to diabetes. She visited, but didn't stay over. Sometimes I stayed overnight with Mom even though Donna was there.

Mom asked for me all the time, which made Donna jealous. But, I explained to Donna that Mom and I spent so much time together even before her illness. I wanted her to understand that Mom and I lived three blocks from each other for a long time. Even after I moved about a mile away, I visited Mom every weekend and lived with her almost every day while she was sick. I began to know what she needed or wanted without her even saying a word. This made it easier for Mom. She didn't have to say anything when I'd come to the nursing home. I would clean her stoma and snap on a new pouch (before the brain cancer, she always said, she hated to be dirty). She almost always had diarrhea, so her pouch would have to be emptied frequently.

One day Donna was sitting in the chair near Mom's bed waiting for me to come after work. Mom said to Donna, "Where is Gail?" Donna told Mom she would get whatever she needed. Mom said, "No, I want Gail." When I finally arrived I went right to work cleaning her up and replacing her pouch. Donna and I took turns going back and forth to the vending machine for candy that night.

Mom had been in the nursing home for a couple of weeks when Mary Anne visited. Donna and I were already there. Mary Anne sat by the window in the wingback chair. Finally she rose to her feet and walked over to the side of Mom's bed. She looked at Mom and said, "Hi, Hazel," like she always did.

Suddenly, Mary Anne started crying. She told Mom she was sorry, but she couldn't hold back the tears. She told Mom she was going to miss her, and it was difficult seeing her like this. Donna held Mary Anne, telling her that it would be all right. I was on the other side of the bed wanting to cry as well, but I managed to keep my eyes dry.

Once Mary Anne left, Donna and I had the chance to talk to Mom about things. Donna asked Mom how she felt. She told Donna that she was afraid. Donna asked why? Mom said, "I never knew anyone who passed on and come back to tell what's on the other side." Donna asked Mom if she was ready and Mom said yes. So Donna said all you have to do is close your eyes and say, 'Lord take me, I'm ready' and God will take you.

For the rest of the afternoon, into the evening, and all though the night we saw Mom's lips ever so slightly repeating the words, "Lord, take me, I'm ready. Lord, take me, I'm ready. Lord, take me, I'm ready. . ." We all settled in for the night. I slept in the chair near the window and Donna in a chair beside Mom's bed.

When we all opened our eyes, it was a bright sunny day. Donna and I walked over to Mom to say good morning. She looked at me, then at Donna, and out the window at the new day and said, "Why am I still here?" Donna said, "That's because your room is not ready yet." The three of us laughed so hard that day.

We cleaned Mom and went to the vending machine to pick up a few candy bars for later. We tried not to leave Mom alone for a long period of time. That evening, everyone visited and stayed late.

While we were there a nurse's aid came into the room to flush Mom's feeding tube. We all looked in amazement when she used cold water from a cup on the nightstand beside Mom's bed. At home, we always used a small amount of warm bottled water. We all looked at each other and assumed the nurse knew what she was doing.

That night after everyone had gone except Donna, Mom started to feel nauseous. Donna quickly reached for the container that we used to wash Mom and placed it under her chin. Mom vomited, filling the container. Donna took it into the bathroom and emptied it. When she returned Mom started over again. Donna pushed the button for the nurse and no one responded. Donna was afraid to leave Mom alone. Finally, after about twenty minutes, Mom was feeling a lot better and was no longer vomiting.

Donna walked down to the nurse's station with the half full pail to ask them why no one responded to the call button. She told them about the vomiting. They said they didn't see the light. Donna, upset, asked to speak with the person in charge, but she was not on duty at this time. After this, we knew it was necessary for someone to be with Mom at all times.

The next morning everyone working in the nursing home that evening knew what had happened with Mom because Donna requested to speak with the head nurse and person in charge. A meeting was set up with the nursing home director, head nursing, and Donna. After the meeting, the staff was more aware and considerate of Mom's needs. We still took turns staying every night. One of the nurses on the floor told us she thought Mom needed a rest from us and that we should not come so often. We disagreed and continued to stay.

Mom's roommate was very quiet, and her daughter often visited. She was raising two children, worked, and took classes. Whoever stayed with Mom also looked out for Mom's roommate also.

Mom was in the nursing home for almost a month now when I decided we should all visit at the same time for dinner on a Saturday or Sunday in the dining hall. I reserved the room for the family to get together in two weeks on a Saturday. This gave everyone time to prepare his or her favorite meal.

When I told Mom I was organizing this, she asked if I could cook turnip greens with the roots cubed in the greens. I said yes and I would also fry some shrimp. She didn't have much of an appetite, and I thought dinner with the family would be good. We all were excited about getting together with Mom. We invited David, who was a person who transported Mom down for x-ray each time she was in the hospital. He also looked after Mom making sure she was okay or if she wanted anything from the store before he left the hospital each day. Also when I was in the same hospital a year before, David had been there for me.

Hardly a day went by that Mom had not spent a day without one of her children visiting. We were always there to keep her company and to make sure she was comfortable and clean.

The day had come for our family gathering, Saturday, March 23, 2002. I went home the night before to go to the store and to prepare to make the turnip greens and fry the shrimp the way I knew Mom enjoyed. Donna stayed with Mom.

I came to the nursing home early the morning of the family dinner so Donna would have the chance to go home, change, and make her salad and I would help Mom get ready. I pulled out clothes from her drawer, laid them on the chair and sat down on the bed beside Mom. We had time to talk and relax before dinner so, that's what we did. After sitting for a few hours I washed and changed Mom then helped her to the side of the bed and this took some time and effort because it was getting harder for her to understand what I was asking her to do. I then helped her into her blouse, buttoned the front then tried to get her into pants, but it wasn't working because of the neuropathy in her feet. She was in so much pain that it was hard to put her foot though the pant leg. After a long time, I decided to just put her in the wheelchair with her blanket around her bottom half and wheel her in the dining room.

When I wheeled her into the dining room, not everyone had arrived but there was still a variety of food to choose from. I wheeled Mom around slowly to see everyone and to say hi to all of her guests. After fifteen minutes, Mom said she was ready to eat. I asked her what she would like, and she said she wanted some of my turnip greens. I asked if she would also like a shrimp or two. She said no, just the turnip greens for now. The greens were still warm; they were packed in an insulated bag. I wheeled Mom closer to the table. She opened the container and ate directly from it instead of putting into a plate. With a small forkful in her mouth, she closed her eyes and chewed. Mom opened her eyes, looked at me, and said, "Tastes like I made them myself," and then she said "you know what to do girl!"

I asked Mom again if she wanted any shrimp and she said, "No thanks, I'm full." She ate all of the turnip greens which I prepared for her in the small Tupperware container. Lately her appetite was decreasing so that was the most I'd seen Mom eat in a long time. I usually fed her with what is on her tray for breakfast, lunch or dinner when I visited but lately, she didn't want to even look at the food. I felt particularly good when Mom said she liked the greens, and I felt even better when she ate what was in the container.

By now, everyone had come and everyone was enjoying the variety of food and I was glad it was being eaten. The family and guests were sitting in chairs around the room talking and laughing and I thought it was a good idea to have this gathering. After everyone had eaten dessert, I noticed the food table was a little messy so I organized the bowls and plates of food still left on the table. Then I walked around saying hi to everyone while people had formed little groups.

I walked over to Mom, who was near the table where she had eaten her greens. She said she was tired and wanted to go back to her room. She didn't say good-bye to anyone because she wanted to leave the room right away. When we got to her room, I helped her undress to get into her bed. Not long after she was settled into her bed, everyone came to her room, a couple of people at a time, to say good-bye. Donna and I decided to stay that night with Mom.

The next morning was also a beautiful day. Mom talked to Donna and me about things that had happened when she was a child and things she did for us when we were young.

We talked for almost the whole day. As I can recall, this was the last conversation where Mom didn't lose her train of thought or forget what she was about to say.

That evening Mom started staring at the corner of the room in the ceiling with a frightened look on her face. Every now and then she jumped as if she was either in pain or she was terrified of someone or something she had seen. We asked Mom what was wrong. She turned toward me and asked, "Why are there so many spiders in the room?" I asked, "What color are they?" she said they are white and they are flying all around me.

Donna was on one side of her bed and I was on the other. I told her they were not spiders, but angels watching over her, then she smiled.

Donna and I settled in for bed since by this time Mom was dozing off to sleep. This time Donna took the chair by the window and I the chair beside the bed. All of a sudden, we heard Mom say something again. Donna and I got up went to either side of Mom's bed. We moved in closer to hear what she was saying. She was calling to her mother. We had never heard her refer to our grandma as "Momma." But, that night she called to her mother as if she was in the room with us. She also called out the name "Frankie," who was one of her cousins who she used to play with when they were children and who had passed away a few years ago.

From that moment on, I felt Mom would be leaving us soon. I knew my mother was closer to the spirit world than with us. I was about to lose my Mom and my best friend.

Each day I visited, I fed Mom until she had enough. Sometimes it was just one forkful and she would be full. Not too long after our family gathering, I requested the feeding tube stopped. I needed to show proof of medical power of attorney for this to happen, which I had, thanks to Tami. Mom was beginning to hate the smell of food because it started making her nauseous. When Cynthia and Donna visited Mom one evening, they brought sandwiches. The smell of the onions made Mom nauseous. Eventually, she didn't want anything by mouth. I knew that her body was not processing food anymore so I didn't force her to eat, and I didn't want the nursing home staff to insist on her having something to eat before they took the tray away after each meal unless of course she wanted it.

Everyone visited Mom the following evening. Nedinia brought a card she had made with a drawing of a tree with all of our names and words to describe Mom. She read it to Mom and Mom said thank you and asked her to place the card on her windowsill for everyone to see. After Nedinia read the card to Mom, she told Nedinia that the, words were so beautiful:

LIVE YOUR LIFE

Life without you will be a difficult task
Just a little more time Lord is all we ask
You have been the adhesive that kept us together
And the warm shelter in stormy weather
You've instilled in us love and harmony
Your accomplishments in life have inspired us so
We will truly miss you, when it's your time to go
The love we have for you cannot be erased
For you are a blessing that can never be replaced
Just remember one thing this is not the end
God has more in store for you our dear friend

With Love,

From all of us

I called Tam on my cell phone. Telling her that we were all with Mom and she suggested we order the urns since we were all together at the nursing home. We all agreed that this was a good idea since Mom wanted to be cremated. We wanted to each have a part of Mom in our own small urns. Tam found a website where we could purchase our urns and she calculated the amount

134

each of us would have to contribute. Donna wanted Tami to use her credit card to pay, but Tam felt uncomfortable placing the order with Donna's credit card. Tami forwarded the website to Donna and Donna's son, Micah, helped his mother place the order later when she got home.

On Saturday, April 6, I was alone with Mom when she had another seizure. They were coming frequently now so I asked the nurse if it was possible to increase the seizure medication, and they said they would. I thought it was important for Mom to be as comfortable as possible at this time.

The next day Lenny stopped by the nursing home early to see Mom. She would return later that day but wanted to visit early to say hi to Mom and to find out if Mom wanted anything when she returned later that day. Before leaving for home, I told her about Mom's seizure the night before since she would be staying with Mom that night. I went home to shower and change clothes. Later that evening, I returned.

When I returned to the nursing home Mom had her room full of people. Nancy and Audrey from the Gut Reaction support group came to visit. Mom told Nancy to come closer because she wanted to say something to her. When Nancy leaned close to her she said to Nancy "I don't want to leave my kids; they are so good to me." Mom didn't realize that Cynthia was beside Nancy arranging her flowers that were on the windowsill. Mom cried after she said this and Nancy gave her a hug and told her it would be all right. Nancy and Audrey didn't stay long and Mom was happy to see them. Vincent was also there; he sat by Mom's side for a while to read the Bible to her.

The next day the nursing staff told me they didn't think Mom had a lot of time left. Mom's roommate was moved out, placed in a different room and another nurse brought in Danish, coffee, bottled water, and more chairs. I called everyone to let them know.

Neil and April came to the nursing home at 11:30 p.m. that night. Neil asked us to step out of the room for minute while he spoke to Mom. Mom was not responding to anyone but he stayed with her in her room for about 15 minutes. We heard him crying as he held her hand and told his grandmother how beautiful her hands were. I went to him, held him, and told him she will be okay.

April then came into the room and said she also wanted to talk with Mom so we gave April time with Mom. Neil and I walked in the room after ten minutes and the three of us reminisced about things Mom used to say and do when we all got together at our family gatherings. Neil said mum-mum was always there for him and she always made him laugh. April started to tear when she spoke about Mom helping her and her Mom with money to continue college, and remembering Mom asking if she could help out with other things she needed while in school. They left at 3:00 a.m. to drive back home to New Jersey.

Monday, April 8, I left work early. The nurse at the home called me and said that Mom was asking for me. Mom had been alone all morning because I had planned to leave work early to visit Mom, and stay with her that evening to give everyone else a break. When I reached Mom's room she didn't say much at first but when I kissed and talked to her the phone rang, it was Tami. While I was on the phone, I noticed Mom seemed restless. I told Tam I had to go to see if Mom needed anything. When I got off the phone, Mom started screaming my name at the top of her lungs. I was startled, because I thought she was dying. She continued to scream, "Gail, Gail, where are you?" I told her I was beside her. She said, "I can't see you." I leaned over the rail to the bed, placed my head on her pillow, and held her as tight as I could. After about 5 minutes, I asked if I could get her something. She said she wanted a glass of iced tea. Mom had a tight grip on my hand, and it was hard for me to reach the nightstand to make the tea. I rang for the nurse and asked for a cup of tea, sugar, and ice. It did not take long for someone to bring the tea bag and hot water. Mom did not like her tea strong so I put the tea bag in hot water for only a second before adding the sugar and ice. I put a flexible straw in the cup and gave it to her. Mom hadn't let go of my arm, so it was a little awkward doing all this with only one hand. I put the straw to her mouth. She tasted it and said, "This is so good, thanks."

That night I slept in the lounge chair with my feet pressed tightly against Mom's bed so that I could feel any movement if Mom needed me. At 4 a.m., I felt Mom's bed shake. Mom was having yet another seizure. I held her tight until it was over, lasting about a minute. I rang for the nurse, who quickly came in the room, took Mom's vital signs, and asked how long the seizure lasted. She gave Mom a drug called Ativan to relax her. At 12:20 p.m. on the same day, Mom had another seizure which lasted 45 seconds.

After the seizure Mom was in somewhat of a comatose state. Her eyes were not open. When I touched her foot by mistake, which usually made her jump, she didn't do anything. I stayed with Mom the whole day, not wanting to leave her side.

> Don't be sad; God is calling you
> Don't be sad; we all must go sometimes
> God is letting you know He's
> ready for you. I hear it's a nice
> place
>
> If you can, let me know and make
> room for me because I'll see you again.

Chapter 10

Final Hours

Nisey was there early Tuesday morning, April 9. I told her about the seizures the night before and I was tired, went home, I took a hot bath and rested on my couch. Donna was there, she stayed at my place every now and then instead of taking the long ride to New Jersey when it was her turn to care for Mom. She prepared a meal for us. After eating, I dozed off for about an hour.

When I woke it was late afternoon and I made dinner. The two of us sat up for a couple of hours talking about Mom and other things relating to her illness. I told Donna I would be staying with Mom again tomorrow, Wednesday.

The next morning, neither of us wanted breakfast. Donna and I where leaving my place and I was about to lock my door when my cell phone rang. It was Nisey calling to let us know everything was OK and that Mom slept well without any seizures. She said I should go to work and that Mom would be okay. But I felt I had to be there for some reason.

I dropped Donna off at the train station, which was within walking distance of my apartment. I stayed with her until she was on the train. Donna wanted to go with me to the nursing home but I insisted she go to work and come in the evening to stay with me. She told me she would be leaving work early that day so I could go home and relax. I thanked her, gave her a hug and she boarded the train.

When I got to the nursing home, I signed in, keyed in the code, and walked through the double door toward room 112B and Nisey was standing outside the room. She told me again everything is OK and that Mom slept well and had a quiet night. Billy had come at 5 a.m. to relieve Nisey in case she wanted to get to work early.

He brought flowers and soft pretzels for the nursing staff. I walked with Nisey to her car out the back entrance as she said again that things were quiet last night and Mom didn't have a seizure and I should go to work and Mom will be fine. But, I had a strong feeling that my place was to be with Mom today.

After Nisey left, Billy and I talked for a while. He asked if I was hungry and I said know but he insisted on getting me something for lunch so I asked him to get me a salad and he suggested the Giant grocery store. He asked me what I wanted in my salad and a few minutes later Billy left. The nurse came into the room, she said her name was Karen, and she will be helping Mom today. Karen was covering Mom's floor since they were short staffed. She said that she had read Mom's chart to familiarize herself with Mom's case.

While asking me if there was anything she could get for me, Karen took a sponge on a stick, moistened it with the fresh water she had brought into the room, and poured the water in a cup on the nightstand beside Mom's bed. She brushed Mom's teeth as Mom's eyes were closed. There was drool on the right side of her mouth. I got a warm washcloth to wipe Mom's face and mouth.

I told Karen I wanted Mom to have her pain medication in about a half hour. That way, it would be working when Mom was moved from side to side while being washed. Mom had two bedsores--one on the back of her head and another on her tailbone. These came from lying in one place too long. Mom was rotated from side to side every few hours. She usually cried out as if they were hurting her whenever the staff washed and changed her gown which made me upset so I usually waited in the lounge until they were finished.

Karen left the room to get Mom's medication. She returned with the medication in an eyedropper. Mom was on her right side facing the window. Karen gently turned Mom's head toward the ceiling, placed the dropper close to Mom's lips, and slowly pushed it into her mouth. When the dropper was in far enough, she squeezed the rubber top.

As the medication released in Mom's mouth, there was a gurgling sound. Karen messaged her throat until Mom swallowed. I asked if Mom was able to swallow the medication. Karen said the gurgling meant she could still swallow.

After forty-five minutes Karen returned with another nurse and it was time for Mom to get washed. Karen asked if I wanted Mom to be on her left side or on her back. I told them on her back would be fine. Then I told Mom I would be down the hall and would be back after they cleaned her up even though I knew she would not respond to what I had just said. I walked down the hall four doors away on the opposite side of the room to the lounge. I watched television, read the newspaper, and then looked out the window.

When I was in the lounge for about 15 minutes I saw Billy walk by and I called to him. He wanted to know why I was not with Mom and I told him she was getting washed. He gave me my salad; we talked for another ten minutes and then he left to get some sleep because he said that he was tired. He asked if I would be all right. I said yes. I thanked him for the salad, he gave me a kiss and a hug, and he went home.

I walked down to Mom's room opened the door to her room which was shut and noticed the curtain drawn around Mom's bed. Karen peeked out behind the curtain and told me that she would come to the lounge to get me when they were finished. I walked back to the lounge and tried to watch television but my mind was not on what was on television but on Mom. After fifteen minutes, I saw Karen standing at the entrance of the lounge. Karen said she told Mom I was waiting and would come to get me. She also said that Mom knew I was there. I thought this was strange, because Mom had not said anything to us since her last seizure. I thanked Karen, took a deep breath and headed down the hall toward Mom's room.

As I walked to Mom's room, for some reason, I felt like I couldn't get there fast enough. When I reached the doorway of her room, my eyes were focused on the windowsill. The sponges and socks that were on Mom's feet before her bath were now off. I wondered why they did not put them back because of the neuropathy they protected her from when the bed linen touched her feet causing her pain. The curtains at the window were completely opened, revealing a beautiful and sunny day. The sun shined in the room brighter than I ever remembered.

The curtain around Mom's bed was not opened all the way. I could not see my mother's face from this angle, only part of her arm and her hands, which were at her side. Mom always liked the curtain around her bed pulled back so she could see anyone entering the room. As I went closer to her bedside, Mom looked so peaceful, lying on her back with her eyes half opened. Even though they were half open, that was wide enough for me to see her staring at the ceiling in the corner of the room.

When I got to her bedside, I gave Mom a kiss and told her how fresh she smells. I went to the phone to dial the number to my job to let my boss, Christa know what was going on and that I was coming to work tomorrow because it would be Donna's turn to stay with Mom but there was no answer. I called the main office front desk and Judy answered the phone. She said she and Vena were in, (who were my co-workers), but Christa had gone on an errand.

As I was speaking to Judy, Mom's eyes shifted from the corner of the room to me, and they were wide open. I said to Judy, "Let me call you back!" I then started, piecing things together...

I hung up the phone, looking into my mother's face. I said, "I love you so much and I know that you have to go, and I will miss you very much. If you can would you come back every now and then to be that angel on my shoulder and keep me in check? I told her that it was okay for her to go because I didn't want her to hurt anymore.

After I finished I began to cry. I placed my head next to Mom on her pillow--the right side of my face touching her left cheek, hugging Mom and holding her tight. I then lifted my head and reached over to get a tissue which was on her night stand to dry my eyes and to wipe her left cheek where I left my tears. I noticed a tear in Mom's right eye and I blotted it then I said, "You understand what I'm saying, don't you?" Then another tear from her left eye ran down her face and followed the track of her laugh line. Her eyes moved to me, and she shrugged her shoulders and her hands that were once at her side were now in front of her with her palms facing the ceiling as if she wanted to say I've got to go . . . I'm sorry. At that moment she took her last breath and she was gone.

I knew Mom was always listening to me though she never responded. It was as if she was locked inside herself. Her face showed no signs of stress after she took her last breath. In fact she looked as if she was smiling. I told Mom I would miss her, kissed her forehead and at that moment, my tears were gone because I felt Mom was in a good place and I was glad she was no longer in pain.

I looked at the clock to see that it was 11:29 a.m. Alone with her, I gave Mom some kisses and a hug. I went outside the room where there was a nurse in the hall. She knew by the expression on my face that Mom had died.

A few minutes later a doctor was in the room taking Mom's vial signs. They marked the time of death at 11:30 a.m. Before leaving the room, the nurse asked if I wanted her to call anyone. I told her that I would make all the arrangements.

Ten minutes after the doctor left the room, my great Uncle Jack, my grandmother's brother, and Aunt Viola, his wife, came to visit Mom. It was hard for the two of them to get around at their ages. Uncle Jack was 91 years old. He had battled prostate and colon cancer a few years ago. It was one of his good days, and he felt like coming to the nursing home. But it was too late, Mom had died and I felt so bad for them. They both walked over to Mom, he touched her hand and then they both shook their heads. Then they sat in the two vacant chairs by the window. The three of us looked over at Mom for a while in silence.

I started calling everyone to let them know Mom had died. Cynthia was first. Donna called an hour earlier to say that she was leaving work to come to relieve me so I didn't bother to call her. When she called I told her that Mom didn't look well. She said she was leaving work, and Marcia, a co-worker would be with her. I called Billy, he had left the nursing home not even an hour earlier but was sitting by the phone in case I called. The news of Mom's death spread fairly quickly and Mom's roommate's daughter Tina came in the room to give me a hug and to tell me she was sorry.

Donna met Tina at the front door when she arrived at the nursing home. When Donna saw Tina she knew then that Mom was gone. She started crying before she got to Mom's room.

Everyone was there by 1 p.m. at Mom's side to say their last good-byes. They all commented on how peaceful Mom looked with a relaxed smile. Uncle Jack and Aunt Viola stayed with us for an hour or so and left.

Someone from hospice came to find out if the funeral director was contacted. I had called them already. When Cynthia arrived, she took Mom's rings off her fingers. There was the wedding band and engagement ring, which belonged to my grandmother; she wore on her third finger right hand, and Mom's band and engagement ring were on her third finger left hand, which she wore even after husband died. Cynthia gave all the rings to me.

Mom was still wearing her watch. As I took Mom's watch off her arm, Donna asked if she could have it. I said yes and gave it to her. Lenny asked me if she could have the blanket that Mom had on her bed to keep her warm. I took the blanket off the bed, folded it, and gave it to Lenny.

Mom, Aunt Viola and Uncle Jack

People from the funeral home came in about an hour after I called to take the body away. We all said good-bye to Mom, and one by one we left the room. Donna asked the person from the funeral parlor if he needed help lifting Mom onto the stretcher. He said no, he would be fine. He did not move her until after we all left the room. He then rolled the stretcher with Mom's body out of the room. We were in the parking lot talking when we saw him put Mom's body in the back of the van and shut the door. I thought to myself, "That was fast."

I dialed Mom's number to let her know what was going on and there was no answer. I finally realized that my best friend was gone, and I will never get a chance to hold, laugh or cry with her again here on Earth. Knowing however, I will talk with her again one day, in the next life however, gave me some comfort.

Before the van pulled off, Donna tried to look in the back window to see Mom but the window was too dark. I was parked beside the van and we were standing outside talking for a while before we got into our cars. The van from the funeral home pulled out of his parking space and drove off.

I called Larry to let him know Mom had died. He kindly asked if I needed him to do anything. I told him no and that I wanted to be with my family, and thanked him. He said to give him a call if I needed to talk. He

also wanted to be notified of the time and place of the
memorial service.

We shared a lot in the past,
more over the last few months
Mom told me she wanted to sleep
but didn't want to die.

I asked if she would look down
on me every once in a while.
She said she would if she could.

Chapter 11
Arrangements

Mom's last request was to be cremated. Soon after her death we planned on having a private service for family members only. Mom wanted a memorial service with her picture at the entrance of the room and for everyone to come together to celebrate her life.

And, that is exactly what we planned to do. There was one problem, though; FedEx lost the urns that we had ordered. Tam had tracked them to one of the carrier's shipping houses. None of us, however, knew where that was. Donna, with Tami's help, finally tracked down the urns. They were delivered to my apartment on Wednesday evening, the same day Mom died and two days before her cremation. They were beautiful and all different colors--white, harvest green and flowery blue. It was nice that everything was falling into place.

It was as if Mom was helping us arrange things from where she was.

That evening Donna and Nisey came to my place to call our relatives and friends to let them know of Mom's passing. They also gave information about the memorial service when we finally figured out the place, which would be the meeting hall in the complex where I live, and time and date of the memorial service.

Things felt to me like they were moving quickly but I was moving in slow motion. Everything around me was moving faster and faster. In a way, I was glad because I wanted this to be over. I kept myself busy making sure everything was set for the cremation on Friday and the memorial service for Saturday.

After Nisey and Donna and I finished contacting most of our friends and relatives, we decided someone should go to the store to pick up food to eat while we sat around reminiscing. Nisey and Donna volunteered to go while I stayed behind straitening up and washing the dishes that had accumulated in the sink. When they returned, they brought with them two pizza pies, beer, and sodas. Vincent came later with Chinese food so we had more than enough to eat.

I was tired so I decided to get out of my jeans and change into something comfortable. I went into my bedroom and put on a cotton pants set, which I thought would feel lighter on my body. I thought about calling Mom, but I suddenly realized Mom was really gone. I couldn't hold back the tears. They kept flowing. My heart hurt so much I dropped to my knees, weeping, and calling out to Mom. I cried until the pain in my heart became less. Vincent heard me cry and came into the room and he held me until I said I was OK.

I got myself together. I told Vincent I would be all right and he could leave me alone. After a few minutes, I was in the living room with Donna and Nisey. Vincent and Donna were drinking beer and talking about old times. I began to feel better. Nisey started watching the basketball game on television with Vincent while Donna and I sat at the table talking about things. Everyone stayed for a few hours and then went home to prepare for Mom's cremation on Friday morning. I couldn't sleep after everyone left even though it was very late. So, I started getting my place ready for my daughter and her family, who were due to arrive the following afternoon. My one- bedroom apartment is too small for five people so I had to move things about to make them as comfortable as possible.

Thursday morning, I was so happy because Tami, Rob and the boys came to visit me at my apartment.

When they finally arrived, they were hungry. Tami and I went out to get lunch. We picked up chicken and mashed potatoes at one of the fast food places in my area, and dropped it off at my place for Rob, Freeman and Isaac. Tam and I didn't bother to eat because we had several things to get for Mom's memorial service.

First, we stopped at Target to get paper to print out the programs Tam had written. We drove to another store to pick up the plates, cups, and flatware, making sure we had enough. While we were driving, Tami thought it would be nice to give seeds of Mom's favorite flowers and vegetables to all who attended the memorial service. They could plant them in Mom's memory, so we stopped by a plant store to pick up the seeds. We were gone for the better part of the afternoon, running here and there trying not to forget anything.

When we returned, Tam and I nibbled on the leftovers from lunch we had brought earlier. I ate the

156

rest of the potatoes, while Tam finished off the chicken. Then we started working on the programs. Tam had already written Mom's obituary at her home and added the finishing touches in the car on her way to my apartment.

It was a good thing we purchased extra paper, because we made lots of mistakes. They were either printed on the wrong side of the paper or it not lining up correctly. Finally, we got it right and were able to print the programs. Tam did such a good job, the program looked so nice. We chose a heavy bond cream paper with a flowery design on the top about 5 inches by 6 inches.

The program had Mom's name on the front with her birth date, date of death, and the time and place where the service would be held. The program was short but laid out nicely.

For the seeds, we printed out and stapled to the seed packs a piece of paper that read:

Live Your Life

For My Grandmother
This lovely flower fell to seed;
Work gently sun and rain;
She held it as her dying creed
That she would grow again.

We worked for hours getting the programs and seed packets perfect. At 8 p.m. it was time for the boys to go to bed. I gave then a kiss, said goodnight. Tam and Rob read a book to them. Then, Rob watched television while Tam and I continued working to complete the programs. By then we were tired and Tam and Rob went to bed about two hours later. I slept on the couch and I stayed up to watch television for a while because I wasn't sleepy.

An hour or so later, I heard voices coming from the bedroom. The door opened and Tam said Rob was having a problem breathing and needed to go to the hospital. I told her I would drive him to the hospital while she stayed with the boys since they were asleep. But, she insisted on taking Rob herself. I called Larry for directions to the nearest hospital. Since he was familiar with the area he gave Tam great directions. They were gone for an hour and a half and when they returned Rob was given an inhaler and was diagnosed with asthma. They went back to bed and so did I, sleeping only two hours.

The next morning, Tam and I got up dressed and drove to the funeral home where Mom would be cremated. Rob stayed with the boys. Mom wanted a small service at the funeral home. All of Mom's children and grandchildren gathered in front of the funeral parlor. Vincent was also there. The funeral director met us at the door and took us to a room with folding chairs. Mom was in the front of the room in a narrow wooden casket. As I walked to the front of the room closer to the body, I noticed Mom was dressed in the pink dress which she wore to Cynthia's wedding per her request. The walk to the casket felt strange. My heart was beating fast and I didn't want to think about or see Mom lying there lifeless but, I wanted to say good-bye again.

After everyone finished viewing the body we suggested Nisey lead us in prayer. According to her will, she wanted Nisey, Billy, and I there to view her cremation. I asked if anyone else would like to stay and Vincent offered. No one else wanted to, and I couldn't do it either. Billy, Vincent, and Tami stayed.

After the cremation we give the urns to the funeral director and decided to meet at Cynthia's place only a block away. They ordered takeout but Tami and I drove back to my place to be with Rob and the boys. We relaxed, watched television, and didn't do much of anything. We did go to the rental office to find out what time I could pick up the key to the hall for the memorial service tomorrow and it was at 8:00 a.m. When we went back to my place we relaxed watch a movie with the boys and it was time for bed.

The next morning the weather forecast called for rain all day, but the sun was smiling in my face when I opened my eyes. We had to pick up the key and go to the hall to get everything all set up.

After picking up the key from the rental office to open the hall door, Billy and Vincent came early in the morning to arrange the chairs and set up the food tables. Since the hall was located in the development where I lived, I was able to see the entrance of the hall from my living room patio. In fact, it was the same hall in which we had celebrated Mom's seventieth birthday. That morning there were lots of fruit and plant deliveries from all of our jobs. Everyone used my address since that is where we all met before the service.

The memorial service was scheduled to begin at 11 a.m. on April 13, 2002. My sisters, nieces, and nephews gathered an hour before at my place. There was a photo of Mom in the pink dress which she wore at Cynthia's wedding on a table at the hall to the reception and a basket on either side of the picture that held the programs and the seeds.

When we all reached the hall, lots of people were already there. I saw my longtime friends Hari, Carolin, and Gloria. Carolin, Hari, and I worked together almost thirty years ago at a battery company and I've known Gloria since elementary school.

Then I saw Larry, who I was glad could make it. Today happened to be his birthday. Somehow, I had managed to remember to send flowers to his home. I went directly over to him to give him a kiss and hug. Carl was also there, and I was glad he was able to come. It was awfully nice seeing friends and family we hadn't seen in a while. I thought to myself it is a shame that we only get together like this for weddings and funerals.

The service started on time. Again, Nisey started things off with a prayer. Tami read the obituary, which she called "Mom's Life." As she read each word I thought to myself, how well Tam knew Mom:

"It would be simple—and all too predictable—for me to re-tell the details of my grandmother's life—to recount the places she had gone—the jobs she held—the date and times of her life's occurrences.

But that would not begin to touch on the significance of the life she led, nor would it ever begin to explain what a soul affects during the course of a life.

I could be a bit predictable—and for anyone who knows me, that would be a stretch—but I could tell you that my grandmother, Hazel, was born and raised as an only child to parents who adored her. She grew into a beautiful young woman—married. And six souls chose her for their mother.

She loved her children. She had a soft heart for animals, flowers, Teddy Pendergrass, contemporary jazz, the casinos—she retired from the University.

Life went on for her, as it does for us all. There were twists, turns, hills, and valleys—the worst and the very best of times.

And now she's gone

That is as far as details go—she was born and now she is gone. But, again, those details wouldn't tell you a bit about her soul—about how she truly affected the lives of those she encountered, and about how her soul could teach so much without even trying.

My grandmother was simple and complex—humble with a flair. She was a gentle woman with a fierce will. And, she had an ability that is so rare—to be gracious and curt when showing disapproval. She held her tongue and spoke her truth with modesty and confidence. She lent her life's wisdom and lessons without ever really giving advice—and while still remaining private.

She taught me about gratitude, and through her friendship, I learned how to embrace life—I learned that I am more than the sum of my challenges—I learned how to connect with my inner strength. I learned a lot about God.

But you wouldn't have known that had I stuck to her life's details."

After Tam finished reading Mom's Life, she surrendered the floor to anyone who wished to share a word. Mom asked Donna before she died to write a poem and to read it at her service. Donna then read her poem titled "Yesterday, Today, and Tomorrow":

Yesterday, I saw myself so small and new while promises come from both of you. While love was all around, tenderness could still be found, and you held your ground. And because of you my life stayed on line, and never could I say that I've been blind. Yes, you did your task and did it well. However, time will tell for troubles and woes we still have to encounter, yet let it be said, your title holds strong, your goals are great you brought me up not a moment too late. And I would not have wanted it any other way but yesterday, today, tomorrow.

Today has gone, passing like a thief in the night, leaving all to wonder of its plight. Has it gone so fast, in just a blink of an eye, can you ask yourself why? Hush as we listen as it speaks, "move over yesterday, for today has arrived." And if by chance it should pass you by, be strong accept with pride and welcome tomorrow for all it's worth for even as it comes, we were all given birth. To know and love the many things around that shaped and formed my life into the person I am today.

Tomorrow let me whisper to you how I've grown. Faith in God is never known until one's love has left their Earthly home. Yes we all must pass on one day yesterday, today or even tomorrow. Hush now, and remember that we are all borrowed. For without the knowledge of existence I will have never known or understood the joys of Yesterday, Today, or Tomorrow. Yes, thank you, my very special person, for sharing with me Yesterday, Today, and Tomorrow. Thank you God for my Mother.

Then it was my turn to read my thought:

Mom, I will miss our quiet times when we used to sit, talk and pick over a box of chocolates.
I will miss our nighttime talks when I stayed over.
I will miss frying up a few shrimp and drinking a cold beer.
I will miss talking on the phone until we ran out of words.
I will miss your call telling me "Your daughter's looking for you."
I will miss calling you when I get home from work, letting you know how my day went.

I will miss you asking me if I heard from Tam and how are the boys.

I will miss those goodnight calls.

I will miss the many things we shared. Most of all, I will miss you!

Mom, I love you. I'll see you again.

After I finished reading my thought, David, Lenny's oldest son, who was very close to Mom told everyone how good Mom was to him. He went on to say that he lived with Mom while in high school because Mom lived near the school he wanted to attend. They formed a special bond. He told everyone in the room how much he would miss her.

Reese, one of our cousins, said a few words. He is the son of my grandmother's youngest sister who died many years ago, also of cancer. Reese grew up with Mom, and they played together as children along with Frankie, my grandmother's older sister's daughter.

One by one, everyone said what he or she thought needed be said. We said The Lord's Prayer together. Bruce, another friend played Mom's favorite song, "What a Difference a Day Makes," on his trumpet.

Lovett, also a longtime family friend, played "Precious Love of Ours" on his saxophone.

When the service was over, everyone ate and gathered in little circles to talk. I was glad to see that Dr. Rolendelli attended along with some of the members from the Gut Reaction Group.

After the service was over, we cleaned the room, broke down the tables, I locked the door and returned my key to the rental office.

We prayed for what we wanted
Not what God wanted us to have.

Chapter 12
Going Home

The following month on Mother's Day it was a bright and sunny day and hard to believe it's a month after Mom's death. While I prepared breakfast for myself, in my apartment, I noticed two birds perched on the rail of my patio. They were so beautiful. I opened my sliding glass door to get closer to them as they started to sing. I grabbed my camera, taking pictures of them from several angles. They didn't stop singing nor did they fly away. They serenaded me for about ten minutes before leaving.

Birds singing to me on Mother's Day.

I felt Mom's presence while the birds were singing. I used to call Mom every Mother's Day and send her a card. In fact, I purchased a card for her a few months before she died. I was so excited and couldn't wait to give it to her. The words inside the card were about girlfriends. They were perfect but I never had the chance to give it to her.

Thinking about the birds, I felt as if Mom had just visited me. I missed Mom so much, sometimes I would cry and pray to God for Mom to come back to talk to me and be with me and comfort me. I watch them until they fly away and then I have my breakfast and relax the rest of the day.

On July 3, 2002, I came home from work not feeling particularly happy and thinking about Mom as usual. I decided to go to the wine and spirit shop to get Godiva white chocolate liqueur, which I always liked but never purchased for myself because it was so expensive. I stopped at the grocery store first to pick up some shrimp, which I also had a taste for. The store was crowded because it was a day before the Fourth of July holiday weekend.

I went directly to the fish counter. To my surprise, the colossal shrimp were on sale so I purchased a pound. I laughed to myself, thinking about the times when Mom and I were not able to eat large portions of food--me, because it was so soon after my surgery and my gut had not healed, and Mom, because she was starting to lose her appetite a few months before she had died. I would ask for just four shrimp at the store. Mom asked if I was embarrassed to purchase such a small amount of shrimp. I'd say "No," since I was asking for what I wanted. Those four shrimp went perfect with fries and a cold beer.

The salmon was also on sale, so I grabbed two pieces. My eyes wandered over to the lobster tails, and I bought two of those. After purchasing the seafood, I headed to the wine and spirit shop where I picked up the white chocolate liqueur. I also purchased a bottle of wine to add to my wine rack that Mom gave me a few years ago that sat on top of my refrigerator.

I started home still feeling a little down and I opened the bottle of liqueur as soon as I was in my apartment and poured a small amount in a fancy glass and sipped. I hadn't eaten much all day because I was so busy at work. My co-worker, Vena, went out to pick up her lunch and brought me back small veggie sandwich on a pita bread, which I nibbled on and stored the rest in the office refrigerator. I had cereal for breakfast so I was getting a buzz from the liqueur.

I decided to call Hari. She lost her dad over ten years ago from colon cancer. Hari and I spoke for a while, and I started crying so hard, I had to hang up. I had to talk to Mom, which I did often because I always felt her presence. I told her how much I would like for her to be here for me, and I wished that she could be here to hold me and take away my pain.

After pulling myself together, I called Hari back. We talked a while longer before saying good night. I went to sleep on my living room sofa until 1 a.m. then went to my bedroom and went straight to bed.

I wake up the next morning to the sound of the phone ringing. It was Tami. I looked forward to our talks more now since Mom's death. We didn't talk long because they were going to Rob's parent's house for a cookout. Robert's parents had moved close to them and were now in Virginia. They had relocated from Florida to a house in Virginia forty minutes from Tam and Rob.

After talking with Tam, I laid in my bed trying to decide what to do for the day. I thought about a workout at the gym, which I often did at least four times a week, and then go to the pool for a swim. It was so hot, and I didn't want to go outdoors unless I really had to.

I turned my head toward the window. My air conditioning was on full blast. All of a sudden, as I lay there, I felt as if my body was being lifted from my bed and taken somewhere. The volume on my television, which I kept low, suddenly seemed loud. I tried to reach for the remote, but I couldn't move my body.

172

Then, everything was quiet; it was dead silence in the room, even the television. I was lying on my back with my hands on my chest. I felt a soft hand touching mine. It was so nice, I immediately felt calm. I heard a voice telling me to open my eyes. When I opened my eyes I saw Mom in front of me. She was wearing a white short sleeve top and what looked like a white skirt. She had a white band in her hair with her hair touching her shoulder. She looked as I remembered her when I was a child. Mom was so young, so beautiful. She told me that she was all right and that she was with her mother. Then she was gone. I was disappointed because I didn't get the chance to talk to her or ask questions. At that moment I knew Mom would always be here for me even though I can't see her.

Mom's last request to us was when we got together for our family dinner at the nursing home was for us to get together on her birthday every year and have a beer on her. Years later we are still keep the tradition. Mom loved life and she always told us to live our life and that is what I intend to do...

I hope and pray that she found that peace and happiness in the next world she was not able to find in this one.

In Loving Memory of Hazel T. Williams

 08/4/1926 – 04/10/2002

And

David Butler, Lenny's oldest son.

06/2/1964 – 06/15/2006

A portion of the sale of this book will go to the Rena

Rowen Breast Center for Breast Center Research.

Photo by Lawrence P. Toto

Gail Felton appeared on the cover of the May/June issue of <u>Health Quest</u> magazine, for looking younger than her years. She also appeared in the <u>Essence Magazine,</u> January 2001 and January 2004 issues of <u>Wisdom of the Ages, Extraordinary people 19 to 90,</u> made an appearance on the ABC TV show <u>The View</u> in March 2001, also on the <u>Oprah Winfrey Show</u> in September 2003. Her hobbies are playing the guitar, dancing, reading, yoga, and exercise.

www.ingramcontent.com/pod-product-compliance
Lightning Source LLC
Chambersburg PA
CBHW021102090426
42738CB00006B/466